1 4 JAN 2017

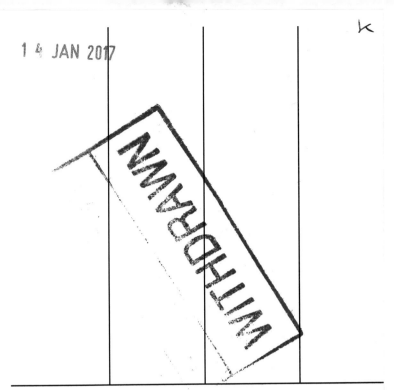

Please return or renew this item by its due date to
avoid fines. You can renew items on loan
by phone or internet:

023 9281 9311
www.portsmouth.gov.uk

Portsmouth
CITY COUNCIL
Library Service

E in my end of year ten history and when I took
another history exam sent by my school over the
holidays and got an A* and 92% I couldn't believe it
and neither could my teac
book!

D1342119

C800606878

☆☆☆☆☆ **More believable than parental advice**

By judith on 6 November 2015

Verified Purchase

My daughter heard about this book from a friend and asked me to get it. Price seemed high but I didn't want to crush her motivation.

Targeted at the GSCE student, not the parent. While i could have shared many of the same techniques with my daughter she has found it more 'convincing' to read them in this book rather than be told by her mother. You need to read through the book from cover to cover to get into his way of thinking - although the basic idea could be written on a side or two of A4 paper! Still, it has been a book we have read together and discussed its application to my daughter and its a good way to show interest and value in what she is doing. The proof so far is that she now has a 8 month chart until the end of GSCEs and a real planned determination to revise - so far so good. I can see that this will/could help her not to panic about the whole thing while she is down in the detail of a topic.

Would recommend for any student/parent needing to have an independent mediator to motivate and devise a plan and approach. Best to get it 8 or 9 months ahead of the summer GCSEs in order to have time to apply his method

⭐⭐⭐⭐⭐ **Very self-motivating**

By SATVINDER SEKHON on 28 November 2015

Verified Purchase

I originally got this book for my son who has been struggling with his gcses. It has really helped to motivated him and change his life for the better and I recommend this to anyone who is having problems revising.

⭐⭐⭐⭐⭐ **This book tells you everything you need to know on how to get great results in your exams**

By Amazon Customer on 6 September 2015

Verified Purchase

This book is the most incredible and inspiring thing I have ever read. It is so helpful and the only book I have found that is both honest and factual about GCSE's. This book tells you everything you need to know on how to get great results in your exams. The level of detail this book contains is what makes it so prefect and will guide you through the process without fault. It's amazing and I recommend it to anyone who is looking for a honest informative and life changing book to help you more than any textbook or teacher will ever. I love it !!

★★★★★ **'These methods work'. Quote from my daughter.**

By debZee on 13 February 2016

Verified Purchase

I bought this for my daughter hoping it might give her some extra tips on revision and some reassurance that she is doing enough from a student's perspective. She is already highly motivated but gets very nervous (as they all do) and sometimes needs a little nudge with regard to organisation. She read the book in one evening and found it very useful. She already knew some of the tips having used them previously with great success but somehow had recently overlooked them. She knows that the methods work and so has begun revision from a refreshed perspective. I bought this in conjunction with a revision planner and she now has her subject timetable all planned out and up on the wall. Although, ideally it would have been better to have bought these a few months earlier, I would say it's never too late and this has given my daughter the extra boost she needed.

☆☆☆☆☆ Brilliant Help

By Sina G. on 18 December 2015

Verified Purchase

Over and over again the book literally described my lifestyle and made me feel like I wasn't the only one going through all of this and in doing so it helped me change myself for the better by making me learn more about my mind. I never got bored and every page opened my eyes. I particularly enjoyed learning about the 'scribble technique' as it has helped immensely.

☆☆☆☆☆ A gift from God!!

By Amazon Customer on 22 January 2016

Verified Purchase

I bought this book in January as i am sitting my exams in May which i was worried about as they're quite soon but needed the motivation and i cant explain how helpful it has been. The revision methods are supposed to be put in place very early but although ive started quite late in January i can already see improvement in my grades. I have just completed mocks and they were 'okay' but feel a lot more confident now as i know i can improve. I am not the most academic but this book has helped me to see that i could be! Highly recommend for anyone needing motivation or revision tips and methods!

★★★★★ **FANTASTICALLY WRITTEN, MOTIVATIONAL AND INSPIRING**

By Amazon Customer on 4 January 2016

Verified Purchase

I found this book through a Facebook post by one of my friends who loved this and said that it helped them achieve A/A*s by the end of the year. I read it and I am in love! It includes the how, when, why, where and what you should be revising as long as loads of methods for different types of subjects. Would recommend this to anyone who would ideally like A/A*s but doesn't know how to get there.

★★★★★ **Highly motivational with very good revision tips**

By winful ezeadum on 26 September 2015

Verified Purchase

I bought this for my daughter in year 11 to help her revise and she absolutely loves it. She says that she likes the revision methods it has and that it has answered a lot of her questions about revising and memorising information. Also, this book is highly motivating for her. Before she got it she used to go straight to sleep after coming home but now, after reading the section about time management and reserving energy she finishes all her homework and revises before sleeping. Overall I can say that I am thoroughly pleased with the results she has gotten so far and hopefully she will get the A*s she deserves by the end of this year thanks to the help of this book.

★★★★★ **It's a small book to easy read, for teenagers who don't have any time ...**

By Sophie B on 9 November 2015

Verified Purchase

Bought for my daughter in October before GCSE as she has early mock exams and it is difficult to get motivated to work as early as october to the GCSE standard.It's a small book to easy read, for teenagers who don't have any time left outside of social network. She has been following the methods straighaway, she works more and she is confident she has a plan, whatever the results will be. I read the book, really interesting, fresh and full of good examples that speak to the 15 year old students. Recommend the spend, I think this is a bit pricey for such a slim book but probably due to success. I think once they have the book the same method applies to A levels.

HOW TO
ACE
YOUR GCSEs

Inspired by Student Success Stories.
We Tell You What Your Teachers Don't.

ANSHUL RAJA

Copyright © 2015 by Anshul Raja
All rights reserved.

Published by Anshul Raja

This book or any portion thereof may not be reproduced or used in any manner whatsoever without the express written permission of the publisher except for the use of brief quotations in a book review.

Printed in the United Kingdom

Cover design by Zahid Pirani

First Printing, 2016

ISBN 978-0-9933488-1-5

How to ACE Your GCSEs
Roberts House, 2 Manor Rd, Ruislip, Middlesex HA4 7LB

www.AcademicUnderdogs.com

To my family Lalit Raja, Amita Raja, Vinod Raja and Sulekha Raja, and my partner Shreena

Contents

Introduction

My name is Raja. For years I struggled with school and exams. It was only during my A-levels where I found a way to stop the cycle of bad grades and disappointment.

In March 2014, I published How to ACE Your A-Levels. It quickly became the number 1 best-selling book in the secondary education category on Amazon as students became aware of my approach to studying, exams and life in general. Within a matter of months schools were asking me to come in to speak with their students. I was even asked to advise teachers on how to help students achieve good grades.

Since the success of How to Ace Your A-Levels, a lot of GCSE students have been contacting me for advice on How to Ace Their GCSEs. So, here we are.

Before we jump into all the important stuff, here's my story...

My story...

I was an average student in an average state school. I wasn't the captain of the debate team, the lead musician at the Christmas play, or the school prefect. My extra-curricular activities included watching television, playing playstation, football and chasing girls.

I got average grades in my GCSE's. However, I always wanted to do well at school, go to a good university and make something of myself. I didn't really see the point of sitting in class for 7 hours a day if nothing was going to come of it.

So for my AS levels, I worked really hard. I went to all my lessons and did my homework. I did everything my teachers told me to.

Two months after completing exams, I went to collect my AS level results. To my horror, I got 3 D's and one U.

I couldn't believe it. I felt stupid. I was angry; angry at my teachers for letting me down, angry at myself for spending so long studying, yet not even being able to get any decent grades. Seeing my friends receiving A's and B's didn't help and I was envious of them. On top of that, I had to tell my parents. I wasn't ready for the disappointment.

After coming back home I went up to my room and felt sorry for myself. I dimmed the lights, sat on my bed, looked down at the floor and thought "What is wrong with me? Why am I so rubbish? Can I blame my genetics? Do I even know what genetics means?!"

I worked so hard, but yet I failed. Was there any point in trying again? What could I do different? It was obvious that I had to retake a lot of exams in June. I realised I had nothing to lose. I had two choices: work hard and maybe get into my desired university which was asking for AAA or not work hard and look for a job. After a push from my parents, I decided on the former, and that I was going to give it one more shot and aim for 3 A's. At least then, if all else failed, in a few years time I wouldn't have to look back and think "if only I had tried".

How could I improve?

School had given me all the information I needed to pass my exams. Yet, I still failed. I knew it was something to do with the way I worked. So instead of reading biology textbooks, I spent a month locked away in my room researching everything to do with exams and revision.

I formulated a handful of simple strategies which I tailored to each of my subjects. I created detailed plans on how to absorb all the information I needed, and achieve, my target of at least 3 A's out of 4 subjects.

One year later, I finished college with straight A grades. At university, I used the same principles and techniques again, and it worked. I left UCL with a first class honours in chemical engineering. My results were in the top 5 percent of the year and I was awarded with a certificate by the Dean of students. Following my AS levels, I have never failed an exam, and I have full faith that I never will.

Since then, I started to share these revision principles and techniques with some of my friends who were struggling with exams. Those who applied the techniques to their own learning, consistently achieved their desired grades. Word about my revision methods started to spread and I began helping friends of friends. Soon I was getting emails from complete strangers asking for help.

Revision technique is key

Over the years, I have perfected my revision methods and designed a programme, which has been tried and tested on many students, with proven results.

The programme has three steps and is designed exclusively for GCSE students. Based on in-depth psychological theory and case based research, it will provide you with the exact guidance on how to prepare, revise and take exams to ensure that you get your desired GCSE grades.

How to use this book

We advise that on the day of reading this book you don't do any revision. Take a complete break and read it from front-to-back. In the early section of the book, you may come across advice which you're familiar with. Please do not be put off by this. I urge you to read further to reap the full rewards of the programme.

Furthermore, take the time to attempt the short exercises. They only take a few mins for each chapter.

First thing's first....

Chapter 1: OMG! GCSEs!?

The transition from year 8 and 9 into GCSEs can be difficult at first. Up till now there has been no real academic pressure, then suddenly everything matters and it's game on. Hearing your parents and teachers start talking about how important GCSEs are can be quite daunting. That's normal and I felt the same way. However, there are some seriously interesting times ahead of you and, contrary to all the 'I hate GCSEs & life' tweets, it can be enjoyable!

The future...

Right, so now it's time to start thinking of the future (feel free to take breath). While this may sound boring and parental, it doesn't have to be! Work and play can be balanced. You can still hang out with friends or play your favourite sport and also do well in your exams!

Your desires will change sooner than you think...

Right now you want to probably just be left alone, play call of duty or want a guy or girl to notice you. That's fine! But your desires will develop into other things. I'm talking about going to college & university. I'm talking about having a well-paid and prestigious career that people respect you for. I'm talking about one day taking care of your parents as they get old. It may seem miles away, but these pursuits will become so important to you in just a few years. For all this to happen, a solid foundation must be built and that is where GCSEs come in!

Chapter 2: What's the point?

What's the point of school? What's the point of doing GCSE's? What's the point of all these exams?

All good questions that I have asked countless people over the years including teachers, politicians and friends. Here's what they had to say...

The teacher...
"These qualifications will improve your prospects for the future."

The politician...
"GCSEs will help you get a good job and therefore a better lifestyle while also contributing to society and the economy."

The friend...
"It will help you get into college and then university. Do you know how many hot girls there are in university!?"

The above answers weren't really good enough for me. I only really found the answer when I sat down to write How To Ace Your A-levels and asked myself the question: I've spent years in education. Hours and hours looking over textbooks and losing hair over exams. What was the point? Was it all worth it?

The answer wasn't immediately obvious but it became crystal clear when I started contacting old friends who had quit education. Apart from the odd few, most of those who dossed during GCSEs and decided to quit had regrets. One close friend opened up to me. He explained that seeing me and other friends on Facebook enjoying college & university made him feel left out and he often found himself asking 'What if?'

After speaking with him, I began reflecting over school, college and university. Never do I look back and think of all the studying or exams. I only really remember the first time experiences, lifelong friends I made and all the laughs we had. To think I had all these experiences while also getting an education! It was definitely worth it & I'm glad I stuck around. As time goes by, you will probably have similar realisations. There's a reason why so many look back on their school days and say "Remember the good old days".

The truth about GCSEs and how they affect your future

If you are someone who wants to push on with the education game and eventually use your qualifications to get a job, then there are some key facts you need to know...

1. Receiving five or more A* - C or 9 – 4 grades, including English and Maths, is often a requirement for taking A-levels or BTECs at sixth form or college.

Nower Hill High School 6th Form Entry Criteria

✓ Students must achieve 6 GCSE passes at grades A*- C. At least 5 of these must be full course GCSEs studied at high school. Two short course GCSEs can be combined to count as the sixth GCSE pass.
✓ Students must achieve a C or above in Maths and a C or above in English Language.

2. Universities look at your GCSE grades to decide whether to let you in or not.

UNIVERSITY OF LEEDS

The minimum GCSE grades needed for admittance to the University of Leeds are a grade C or above in English along with two other subjects at grade C or above (applicants will also need a minimum of two other level 3 qualifications).

Some programmes, however, do have GCSE requirements above this minimum, for example, medicine, healthcare programmes, dentistry and business programmes. It is therefore important to ensure that students check **all** the entry requirement information as any GCSE requirements will be made clear at this point.

3. If you want to be Doctor, Dentist or Vet then many universities have higher minimum requirements often asking for As & A*s (7s, 8s & 9s) in multiple GCSE subjects.

Qualification name: Medicine

A level offer: AAA

Required subjects: A in chemistry and biology at A level; third A level at grade A in any subject except general studies and critical thinking; at least six GCSEs at grade A including chemistry, physics and biology or double science; GCSE grade B in English and maths.

4. Many other high paying jobs ask for a minimum GCSE grade usually for English and Maths.

The exact qualifications you'll need will depend on the programme you apply for. But here's what we usually look for:

Grade B or above for GCSE Mathematics and English Language

300 UCAS points or equivalent (excluding General Studies and re-sits)

2.1 degree in any discipline.

5. Being accepted into a top grammar school or 6th form college can enhance your chances of receiving an offer from a top university. Top schools have special relationships with universities which can help when submitting your application. This has been quite controversial over the years and there has been pressure

placed on universities to stop this favouritism, but it still exists.

I'm 15 years old & have no idea what I want to do in the future

At your age, there is no way anyone can expect you to know what you're doing with your life. I changed my mind several times over the years. One minute I wanted to be a doctor then, after watching a few episodes of CSI (Crime Scene Investigation), I decided that I wanted to be a forensic scientist. At college I settled on Chemical Engineering which I studied at university. Then I changed my mind again and dived head first into asset management and commodity trading!

The point is your mind will probably change too. That is why you need to keep your options open and the only way to do that is to achieve the best possible grades you can at GCSE.

What is the point of learning this nonsense? I'm never going to use it anyway.

Learning stuff that I thought I'd never use like Pythagoras's theorem and biological cell mitosis really used to bother me during GCSEs. I used to constantly complain to my mates and say "Why can't they teach us something useful and interesting? Like how to design video games and make lots of money"

It's only now I appreciate that even though what we were learning was irrelevant, there was a reason for it. I found four benefits of participating in this cycle of schooling, studying and exams:

1. **Learning how to teach yourself** – Yes you have teachers who help you along. However, over time you have to teach yourself. This not only means building learning processes to store information in your head, but also developing ways to find information on your own without

a teacher telling you where it is. This is a skill you will use for the rest of your life.

2. **Finding out what you're good at** – You have to try everything to find out what you excel at and are truly interested in.

3. **Assembling proof** – Your GCSEs aren't just letters written on a piece of paper. They are written in stone. Well not actual stone but in permanent records that will enable you to show others how good you are and slap proof on the table. Proof that you're a determined person who doesn't back down from a challenge. Proof that you can set yourself a target and find a way to get there.

4. **Building mental discipline** – Sacrificing what you want now for what you want eventually. This is my definition of mental discipline. I don't know anyone who hasn't found it hard to sacrifice things to study, particularly during high school. I know people who have built good mental discipline and others who haven't. When I compare the lifestyle and wellbeing of both groups, it's like they are on different planets.

Hopefully this shows you that school is far more than solving maths problems and learning about onomatopoeia. It's more than impressing the hot guy/girl or getting sent to detention. These years shape who you will become in the future and the choices you make now will determine if you will become a great person or an average Joe.

Some stats...

The fact that you're reading this book probably means that you want to do well in your GCSEs. However, if you're on the fence or sceptical about how GCSEs can help you, take a look at the stats below. It's no surprise that those with GCSE's generally earn more income than those who don't. The table below shows that the average person with a decent set of GCSE's earns 20% more than an individual has no qualification.

Data summary

Average hourly pay - 2010

Qualification	Median hourly pay (£)	Pay gap to GCSE, %
Degree	16.10	85
Higher education	12.60	45
A Levels	10.00	15
GCSE grades A*-C	8.68	0
Other qualifications	8.07	-7
No qualification	6.93	-20

SOURCE: ONS

Why should I sacrifice my time now for a future that does not exist yet?

One of the problems in high school is that you can be cool or popular without being smart. More often than not, the class joker or bad boy/girl are usually the cool ones. At many schools, being smart is actually seen as being uncool. However, overtime, coolness will depend more and more on how smart you are. At some point over the next few years, you'll stop hearing the words 'cool' and 'popular' and they will be replaced by 'respected' and 'successful'. Those with prestigious and high paying jobs will generally be seen as attractive, respected and more popular. Given that you will want to be cool for say 3 or 4 years but want to be successful for 30 or 40 years, isn't it logical to make a sacrifice now? I think so.

8

Cool vs smart

You might be thinking – why can't I be cool and smart? You most certainly can but you have to define what cool is. If being cool to you means being the rebel and class joker then it will be difficult to focus in school as you constantly have to keep up your reputation. However, there is a way to stay on top of the social food chain without coming across too keen in class. <u>Just don't let anyone know how hard you're working</u>. When you put in several productive hours after school and achieve full marks in a class test, don't boast about it the next day. Make it seem effortless and have everyone assume you're a natural genius! Trust me it helps.

This is an interesting topic which I could write about for pages & pages, but that's not why you are reading this book. You're here to learn how to smash your GCSE exams with the best grades you can possibly get. I'm going to show you how to do this in my 3-step plan. However, it's important you understand the social dynamics in high school, see how your grades impact your life 5, 10, 20 years down the line and appreciate how your desires will change.

It's a bit lame to quote Ashton Kutcher but I have to admit, he hit the nail on the head with this one...

"The sexiest thing in the entire world is being really smart. And being thoughtful. And being generous. Everything else is crap! I promise you! It's just crap that people try to sell to you to make you feel like less. So don't buy it. Be smart, be thoughtful, and be generous."
-Ashton Kutcher

Chapter 3: Who is to blame?

During my GCSEs, I spent hours daydreaming about how I wanted to learn how to drive, go to college and university. I just wanted to get away from the constant stress of being around my parents because of their high expectations surrounding my grades. At times, I was more worried about not disappointing them than thinking about how GCSEs would help shape my life.

Regardless, the high expectations of my parents and the fact that I wanted to move out and stand on my own two feet was enough motivation for me to accept the sacrifices I would have to make. My issue, however, was that I did not believe I would be able to get the grades I wanted. This was because I made these excuses:

1. My school is rubbish
2. I can't motivate myself
3. I'm not smart enough

Sound familiar?

Looking back, I made these excuses because I didn't fully believe in myself and my ability to achieve high grades. Finding out that they simply weren't true was the first step towards improving my results.

Don't stop, believing...

Let's face it, everyone has the capability to sit down and work, but it's our psychology and our individual personalities which hold us back. This is a well-studied area. Let's talk about the well-known psychologist, Julian Rotter, who introduced the locus of control theory.

"Locus" which is Latin for place or location, is defined as either *external* or *internal*.

- External locus of control: when an individual believes that what happens in their life is caused by environmental factors which they cannot influence.
- Internal locus of control: when the person believes they can control their life.

If you have the right locus of control, you will be successful in your exams.

Try this...

To find out whether you have an external locus control or an internal locus of control, write down the top three reasons why you think you won't succeed in your exams. Really think about it and be honest.

Were your answers along the lines of:

A

- I don't have the natural intelligence to do well, therefore it is out of my control
- My teachers are rubbish
- My school doesn't give me proper guidance
- There isn't enough time

Or:

B

- I don't work hard enough.
- I don't revise the right material
- I don't start early enough

If your answers were more in the A category, you have an external locus of control. If they were more in the B category, you have an internal locus of control.

Don't blame your environment!

Having a high internal locus of control is important to achieve top grades. If you have an external locus of control, you will believe that your environment (e.g. your school, natural intelligence, teachers) is why you will fail. As these factors are not in your control, you will believe that doing well in your GCSEs is impossible. Therefore, you will feel that there is no point in even trying to work towards your exams.

Don't shoot yourself in the foot before even starting!

Your locus of control is not set in stone. It is something that can be changed, and once you have crossed that bridge, you will never look back. Getting your desired grades will become easier!

In order to believe that your grades are in your own control, you must alter your mind-set and stop using external locus of control excuses. Over the next few chapters we will discuss these external loci excuses and prove how little impact they have on your grades.

Chapter 4: My school is rubbish

There are three different types of schools in the UK. These are private, grammar and state schools. I've attended all of them at different times during my education and despite what all the inspectors say, there are some big differences between them. The two main differences are student culture and quality of teachers.

Student culture

"Boffin"…"Teachers pet"…"Geek"

Heard these before? These are all names students get called if they are high performers. Let's face it smart kids getting picked on is no new topic – you see it everywhere. We've all seen the American teen movies where the 'jocks' are at the top of the food chain and 'nerds' are at the bottom. The same social boundaries occur at schools in the UK. However, through personal experience and research these boundaries were more dominant in state schools.

The state school…

I'm talking quite generally here, as I know there are a bunch of excellent state schools with great culture. However, the culture of the state schools I personally attended, put me off working hard and obtaining good grades.

Being smart and doing well was either un-cool or not important. School was more of an inconvenience and everyone went to great lengths to display how little they cared about getting good grades. In a culture like this, it's very difficult to ignore the crowd and focus on doing well. My experience at grammar school was very different.

The private & grammar school...

During the first few weeks of grammar school, I was shocked to see how much of a level playing field it was. There were nerds and jocks just like every other school but there was one key difference - being smart was not 'un-cool'. Most people openly displayed their desire to do well and go on to achieve great things at college and beyond. Over time I learnt that this was not unique to my grammar school. Many students I mentored from similar schools were familiar with the same culture.

It's this culture that helps private and grammar schools dominate the top of league tables year after year.

I don't go to a grammar school and my parents can't send me to a private school. So why should I bother?

My intention wasn't to make you feel hopeless or at a disadvantage to other students. It's to help you understand how much school culture can influence your ability to achieve top grades. Understanding this will help you ignore those who desperately try to show everyone they don't care about school and exams. Freeing yourself from these negative influences and learning how to work by your own standards is the first step to achieving top grades.

Quality of your teachers

It's always helpful to have a good teacher especially for subjects which require oral exams and lots of essay writing, such as English. So, what makes a good teacher? In order of importance a good teacher is someone who...

1. Can control the class
2. Knows their subject inside out
3. Can explain complex concepts in a simple & digestible way

14

4. Ensures that the full syllabus is covered multiple times before exams
5. Inspires and motivates their students.

Having gone to state, private and grammar schools there were some teachers who were great and ticked all 5 boxes while there others who didn't tick any! The point is, regardless of what school you go to, the quality of the teacher you end up with is out of your control and blaming them for poor grades just isn't going to help. Every year I hear GCSE students make these kind of remarks...

"My teacher couldn't control our class so we only covered half of the syllabus – I'm going to fail!"
- *Stephanie*

"Throughout the year we kept getting homework that has nothing to do with our exams. Now I don't have enough time to revise everything we need to know"
- *Amar*

It's easy to think that having good teachers result in good grades and bad teachers result in bad grades. However, this simply isn't true. Far too many students rely on the quality of teachers and lesson time. I fell into this trap too and whenever I didn't understand something I would tell myself:

"The teacher clearly hasn't explained this properly because I don't understand a thing"

During study sessions, I'd use this excuse to skip over the hard stuff instead of persevering. It's only after I stopped blaming teachers, did I start figuring things out for myself and perform better.

Teachers and lessons are just one tool out of many in your tool box that can help you achieve top grades in your exams. There are other more effective tools you can use outside the classroom. In the 3-step plan, I will show you learning techniques that you can use during your personal study time and describe how they can be more effective than any classroom session.

Chapter 5: I can't motivate myself

Being able to sit down at your desk each day and get some work done for a few hours in theory doesn't sound very difficult to do. However, for some reason, most of us find it hard to get going and drift off into lala land after reading just a few lines. During GCSEs, I remember wondering whether this difficulty was unique to me or whether everyone else had a hard time as well. I often asked – Why was it so difficult to motivate myself? What are the causes?

I just have a short attention span

An average person's attention span lasts around 10 mins. Add some fluctuating hormones along with noisy siblings and you can get away with a 5 minute span. Halve that again and you more or less get my attention span at the age of 16. At the time, I was convinced I had ADD (Attention Deficit Disorder) a psychological condition that prevents people from concentrating. In fact I went to the doctor at one point to check, but my suspicions were wrong. Even after this check-up, I still felt my poor attention span was completely out of my control and that I'd need a miracle to ever get anything done.

I don't have enough energy

Does this look or sound familiar?...

Demise Swift @demislouises
I'm too tired to do coursework or revise. #Sleepy #Tired #ThinkImAnaemic #NeedMoreIron

Elijah Ofon @elixofon
How am I supposed to concentrate after a long day of school. Don't teachers understand!!?" #Bed #NeedForSleep #NeedForSleep2

We're all familiar with that tired and droggy feeling. Reading a few lines of your science text book feels like printing a page with no ink in your printer – you read the words but nothing sticks.

Sometimes it can feel like our minds run on batteries. Every morning we wake up with a set finite amount of energy for the day. When it runs out, no more intense thinking can be done and only sleep can charge the battery and energy stocks.

Let's do this!   R.I.P

Can we change our attention span and battery life?

Over time I realised that both attention span and energy levels can be improved gradually. However, it requires pushing yourself to do a little more than you did the previous day. Doing this enhances your mental stamina. Let's use an analogy of Stacey the marathon runner to make things clearer...

Stacey decided to run a 10km marathon in 9 months time. Having never run this far before, she started training and on her first day reached a distance of 2km in 50 mins before running out of energy. She felt disappointed and started to think she wasn't cut out for running. However, she decided to keep trying. For days she struggled – 1.9km:51 mins; 2km:54 mins; 1.8km: 52 mins. On the fourth day she got herself to 1.8km in 49. She felt like her energy was running out again but somehow found a way to push on to finish at 2.1km in 51 mins. By constantly pushing to run a little further and faster each time, she built up her stamina to a point where she could complete the 10km marathon in good time.

Is training for athletics any different from revising for an exam?

No. It took me years to believe this but our minds are just like muscles that can be conditioned to last longer and work more effectively. Just how Stacey pushed to do 100m more, you can push to do one page more. Over time you'll be able to work for longer periods of time without feeling droggy all the time.

This stuff is boring. I'm not interested enough to learn about it.

It's clear that you need to be interested in something to actually be motivated enough to sit down, concentrate and learn it. However, you also need to spend time learning it to give yourself a chance to be interested. This is why it's important to get stuck in and give every subject a chance.

I can't motivate myself. Summary...

It's easy to treat attention span and energy levels as external loci of controls. However, it is a variable that can improve with mental exercise. More will be discussed on the topic of motivation in step 3 of our proactive plan.

Chapter 6: I'm not smart enough!

Intelligence is a word that's thrown around a lot. So here's the official definition of it and the one I am referring to from this point onwards:

The ability to acquire and apply knowledge and skills.
-Oxford Dictionary

Yes there are different types of intelligence like social intelligence which is the ability to read peoples' behaviour. However, the intelligence I'm referring to is the one that helps you to learn and understand new information. Essentially the intelligence that helps you achieve good grades.

Let's talk about intelligence...

My intelligence has always been average. I have never been able to grasp concepts easily or memorise something by reading it once. I completely failed my AS levels, but when it came to my final year, I left with straight A's.

Did my natural intelligence suddenly increase in one year or was it really that my intelligence played a small part in achieving my desired grades?

I, like many, used to get frustrated that there seemed to be lots of 'naturally' intelligent people among my peers. Some of my friends seemed to just 'get it', understanding and absorbing information with much less effort than what I put in. I used to think that I would not be able to achieve the same grades as them. However, I came to realise that intelligence was only one small part of the formula for success. **Study technique** and **mental discipline** were actually far more important...

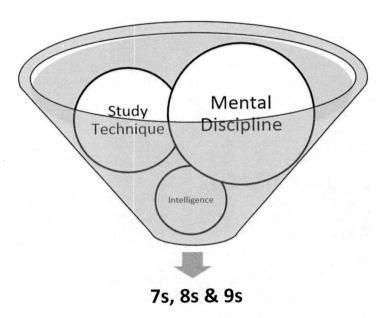

7s, 8s & 9s

Intelligence vs mental discipline...

For me, personally, as soon as I stopped worrying about my own intelligence and started focusing on mental discipline my grades improved. I realised that cursing my intelligence was pointless because it was a constant that I was born with and couldn't change. However, mental discipline was a variable that I could improve to make up for my lack of intelligence. This poker analogy highlights my point...

"The measure of our future success and happiness will not be the quality of the cards we are dealt by unseen hands, but the poise and wisdom with which we play them. Choose to play each hand to the

best of your ability without wasting the time or energy it takes to complain about either the cards or the dealer or the often unfair rules of the game. Play both the winning and the losing hands as best you can, then fold the cards and ante up for the next deal!"
-- Joe Klock

Next time you're in class, take a look around. You should be able to categorise yourself and your classmates into those with average and high intelligence. You can also separate them according to mental discipline...

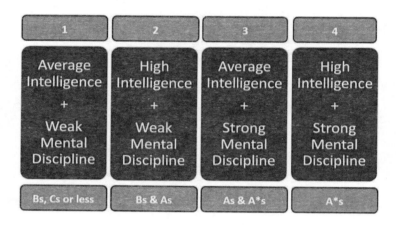

1	2	3	4
Average Intelligence + Weak Mental Discipline	High Intelligence + Weak Mental Discipline	Average Intelligence + Strong Mental Discipline	High Intelligence + Strong Mental Discipline
Bs, Cs or less	Bs & As	As & A*s	A*s

Even though there are other factors that affect a student's ability to achieve good grades, the above model is a good rule of thumb. I used to sit in column 1 and constantly achieve D's and E's with the occasional C or B. However, I moved over to column 3 after improving my mental discipline and study technique.

Study technique...

From mentoring hundreds of students, I've found that many see study technique as a red herring when in fact it isn't. Using the correct study technique is the key to studying <u>efficiently</u>. Using the right techniques from the start will allow you to get in, store or understand all the information you need and get out so you can relax and do whatever you want afterwards. Step 1 of our 3 step plan will provide every technique you need to help ensure you're fully prepared for your exams.

I'm not smart enough. Summary...

Before you can truly benefit from my advice in this book, you need to stop telling yourself that you can't do it because "you're not smart or intelligent enough". It's like complaining that the sky is blue. As soon as you let go of your constants (intelligence) and focus on your variables (mental discipline & study technique), remarkable changes will occur. You will be able to achieve anything you sent your mind to. Trust me!

The three
step plan...

Chapter 7: How to achieve your desired grades

During GCSEs, I had been a D and E grade student who had high hopes but very little self-discipline. Over time I became bitter and angry at myself for constantly falling short. Until one day, after receiving another set of bad exam results, something changed inside me. Enough was enough. I was sick and tired of seeing my parents and friends pity me, teachers not take me seriously and receiving rejection letters from good schools.

This anger was the fuel I needed to break out of my unproductive cycle of trying and failing. Over time I found a way to get the devil on my shoulder to shut up and I started listening to the angel which was telling me to 'Act Now!' This was my 'turning point'.

Looking back, I now realise that there are two types of people who exist.

1. Pro-active: those who would revise throughout the year.
2. Reactive: those who would wait until they *had* to revise.

Pro-active vs. reactive

During my early years and prior to my 'turning point' I would wait until the very last moment, when the exams or coursework deadline was looming before studying. The looming deadline would be my motivation to study. I realised that this wasn't just about exams: it was every part of my life. I wouldn't clean my room until my parents threatened me with no TV. I wouldn't install anti-virus software until my computer stopped working. I would leave my ironing until the morning before school. I wouldn't shave for an entire week until I had a Biology class, because I knew that my Biology teacher (ex-army) would make me clean up litter for the entire lunch time if I wasn't clean shaven. The school bus stop was 10 minutes away from my house. To make the bus on time, I'd wake up 20 minutes before, just because I *had* to. If I stayed in bed, I'd have to walk an extra 20-30 minutes to catch a train and then walk up an enormous hill. I am ashamed to say that I missed that bus at least once a week, just because I wanted those extra minutes in bed, and I knew that I didn't technically *have* to wake up: after all, I could still get to school by train!

Looking back, I cringe at how completely 'reactive' I was. My motivation to be productive solely depended on certain situations and circumstances which forced me to be productive. If there was no pressure, I would get nothing done.

The benefits of being a pro-active person

After becoming fed up of failing at school, I decided to get rid of my reactive ways and attempted to be pro-active. Instead of ignoring and pushing looming deadlines to the back of my mind, I would face them head first. Rather than waiting around for the inevitable deadlines of exams and coursework, I would plan for these. I would iron my clothes and shave the evening before, and wake up those few minutes earlier. Having been both a reactive and proactive person, I can honestly say that being pro-active is so much less stressful: you are not constantly rushing, worried and pressurised to meet the next deadline. Instead, you are working at a relaxing and manageable pace.

Academic study was still challenging, but I had time to enjoy other activities such as meeting friends, going to the cinema, swimming and going on dates. This was much more enjoyable as I didn't feel guilty or fear upcoming deadlines and exams, as I had already planned for them as opposed to ignoring their existence as I did before.

It was this realisation and change in my mindset that allowed me to create a pro-active plan to achieve top grades. This plan forced me to face deadlines. It consisted of simple strategies in each of my subjects to prepare myself, so that I learned almost everything I needed for my exams.

I started from scratch, pretending it was the start the year, and took no shortcuts in spite of obvious time constraints. At this point, I knew that I wanted top grades and I knew why. I wanted to go to a good college or 6th form, a top university, study a top degree and land a high paying job. All I needed was a strategy. It was then, I produced the proactive plan...

The Pro-active plan

In this plan, there are three main steps that any student must go through before they take their exams:

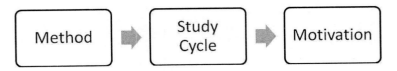

1. **Method (Chapter 8):** This section contains all the no nonsense advice provided for students by students. I introduce the most effective, simple technique for learning information for exams. This section also includes exactly what to revise and how to plan your revision.

2. **Study cycle (Chapter 9):** What exactly is hard work? Everyone tells you to do it but no-one really explains what it is or how to do it. I believe hard work is a skill in itself and has to be practised. In this section, I'll compare the day-to-day habits of successful and unsuccessful students to help you gauge how much work is enough.

3. **Motivation (Chapter 10):** This section is the 'fuel' for the study cycle. Here I show you how to push yourself to study on a day-to-day basis, so that you have the energy and enthusiasm to execute the concepts in step 1 and 2.

Chapter 8: Step 1 - Method...what the A graders don't tell you

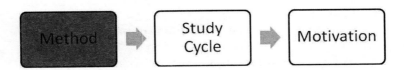

By the end of this chapter you will know **when, what** and **how** to revise for your exams. All of the methods described here are those I have personally used to consistently achieve top grades (often 90%+) in exams. Some of the content is controversial, and your teachers may not agree with my concepts. However, these concepts have been tried and tested on many students and have never failed me or anyone I've taught them to.

When...

Many students switch off when it comes to devising a strategy on when to revise, as they feel time would be better spent actually revising. My response to this is simple...

Direction is more important than speed!
-Me (Anshul Raja)

Each year I come across hundreds of students who are going nowhere very fast. At this moment of time, you might be one of them. So how do you start running in the right direction? The answer is simple: by having a clear and proven plan that stops you from second guessing yourself. One that stops you constantly worrying if what you're doing is correct. The 'when' section will help you achieve this by helping you plan the best path to achieving top grades.

What...

So you've got a revision plan. Now what? Textbooks, revision guides, notes, hand-outs, slides. Some schools tend to chuck all this information at you, and expect you to just soak it up like a sponge. This doesn't happen! Furthermore, the 'one size fits all' revision guides and online tools filled with colourful pictures just add to the confusion! So what do you use and what do you ignore? This section will answer just that by showing you what <u>learning material</u> you need use to achieve the highest marks in your exams.

How...

Once you find out when and what to revise, how do you get it all into your brain and get it to stick? To do well at GCSEs you'll need to spend several hours a week in front of your books. I know, it sucks. However, while you're there you might as well work properly and efficiently. By this, I mean reading through your learning material, absorbing the important information and being able to use it when needed. There's a special method that can help you do this. I call it the 'scribble technique'. I'll show you how to use this and compare it to other techniques to help you understand why it's so effective. Furthermore, I'll show you a few study tricks you can use to further enhance your chances of achieving top grades.

Let's get started...

Chapter 8a: When to revise?

The most common and detrimental assumption made by students is the following:

"I'm not going to start revising now because I'll forget everything before the exam anyway".

This was always my excuse for not revising and it's hard to not believe any different, because information is so easy to forget. If in one month's time, I asked you to write down everything you remember from this book, chances are you'd struggle to regurgitate 10% of all the information. This is why intense cramming before the exam seems like a logical approach.

However, what I and many other students failed to recognise was that intense learning close to exams doesn't really help you remember that much either. Furthermore, cramming simply isn't practical because most of the exams are bunched up too close together. Even if they weren't, for a person who doesn't have a photographic memory, a few days is just not enough time to effectively retain all the information you need to achieve an 8 or 9.

When should I start revising?

We all know what revision time tables are, but the real question is - When should I start revising? The answer is and always will be 'as early as possible'. This is easier said than done and I know many students don't even think of exams or revision until April or May comes around. Using this approach will only make life harder so it's important that you start preparing for your exams from the word go. I cringe while I write this because I remember how I reacted when my parents told me to start preparing in November for exams in May. I didn't listen. However, if someone sat down with me and showed me how to spread my exam prep evenly over several

31

months, I would have probably done it. This is exactly what I'm going to demonstrate to you by showing you a conversation I had with a GCSE student called Beth.

Beth...

Beth was in her final year of GCSEs. She had completed some modular exams in year 10. However, having achieved C's and D's, she wanted to retake them in the upcoming year 11 exams. Six months prior to her exams, I went to her house and we got talking about GCSEs. Our conversation went something like this...

Me: *"So how are you preparing for your exams in May?"*

Beth: *"I'm just trying to keep up with my homework and pay attention in class"*

Me: *"Are you really?"* (Sarcastically)

Beth: *"Yes! I'm really trying this year!"*

Me: *"Fine I believe you, but have you started preparing for your exams and revising?"*

Beth: *"Doing the homework and stuff is preparation right?"*

Me: *"Unfortunately not. Homework does help but the majority of the work required to achieve top marks has to be done in parallel to what your school sets you"*

Beth: *"How do you mean?"*

Me: *"Most GCSE subjects require learning large volumes of information and this can only be done through self-study and learning in layers"*

Beth: *"OK. So what are layers and how do I learn in layers?"*

Me: *"I'll explain it to you but first you need to understand how our memories work..."*

Memory – the virtual filing cabinet

I explained to Beth that our memories are like virtual filing cabinets. When you learn something for the first time, a fraction of that information is filed into place. Over time, the information in the filing cabinet becomes mixed around and unorganised. However, when you re-learn the same set of information you add more to the file and reorganise the whole lot. After each repetition or layer, the more information you add and the longer it stays organised for. The graph below is an example of how applying 4 layers of learning over 40 days can help you retain close to 80% of what's required.

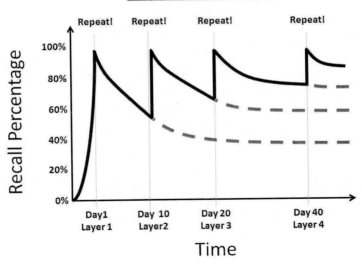

Forty days is cutting it quite thin for GCSEs as there are so many exams to do. For all the exams I've done, I performed best in the ones where I completed the first layer 2/3 months in advance. Even when I was only able to complete a second layer maybe a week before the exam, I would still achieved marks close to 100%. This is the benefit of starting early and using layered learning!

Beth: *"Right. I understand why it's important to start early and spread the revision over time in layers. Can you help me plan my revision schedule over the next few months? "*

Me: *"Sure…"*

The layered learning timetable – layer one

Beth was doing 10 GCSEs and had a total of 20 exams starting in May the following year. This was the first layer time table I made for her, starting first November.

Layer one			
Subject	**Start date**	**End date**	**No. of days**
Mathematics	1 November	14 November	14
English Language	15 November	28 November	14
English Literature	29 November	12 December	14
Biology	13 December	26 December	14
Chemistry	27 December	9 January	14
Physics	10 January	23 January	14
Geography	24 January	6 January	14
German	7 January	20 February	14
ICT	21 February	27 February	7
Textiles	28 February	6 March	7

Beth: *"Why 2 weeks per subject? Is that enough?"*

34

Me: *"Every subject and person is different so it is difficult to estimate how long it will take you to complete the first layer. However, from my own experience and from mentoring many GCSE students, two weeks is a good rule of thumb for most subjects."*

Beth: *"Why have you only allocated 7 days for ICT and Textiles?"*

Me: *"This timetable is for your exam preparation only. Most of the marks for Textiles and ICT come from coursework or controlled assessments. Given that each of these subjects only require one exam in the summer, you won't need as much revision time compared with the other 8 subjects."*

Beth: *"Some of my subjects have multiple exams. For example Biology has 3 written exams. Would I have to cover the material for all 3 exams across 14 days?"*

Me: *"Yes – that's right. You'll have to allocate 4/5 days per exam. The sciences can take longer to revise for than the other subjects so feel free to add on some time. Remember – the revision time table is not set in stone and is more like a guide to help keep you organised"*

Beth: *"Do I have to do one subject at a time?"*

Me: *"I preferred studying one at a time as I wanted to explore each subject as thoroughly as possible before moving on to the next one. However, many students prefer completing all the subjects together so they can stay 'in tune' with class, homework and coursework. No matter how you do it, the important point is that by the end of layer one, you should have thoroughly understood each subject."*

Caution!

There was one point where, instead of completing one subject at a time, I decided to complete the first layers alongside classroom lessons. Every time my teachers set homework on a topic, I would use my textbook and handouts to complete the first layer before taking a stab at the homework. Unfortunately, some of my teachers were unable to control the class and as a result we didn't finish the syllabus in time for exams. This came as a bit of a shock as no one gave me or anyone else in my class a heads up. Unfortunately, there wasn't enough time to finish the rest and I got a C in the exam. Had I stuck to my own layered learning time table, I would have been prepared and achieved a much better result. It goes to show that sometimes you have to take matters into your own hands!

Beth: *"Are you sure I won't just forget everything I did in November?"*

Me: *"Yes – I'm sure! But if you don't believe me, test it out for yourself. Choose a chapter from a text book and read through it as you would during revision. Leave it for a week, and then read through the chapter again. How much easier was it to grasp and remember the principles? How much less time did you have to spend to learn the same facts? If you repeated this again in a few weeks, you will be able to skim read the chapter in a mere fraction of the time and all the information will come back to you instantly.*

When you reach layer three, skim reading through your textbook should jog your memory in the same way. This is when you know you are fully ready for the exam."

Layer one – What you need to know

The first layer is the most important one of them all. It also takes the longest to complete because it's the first time you are learning the material outside of class. So if you find yourself spending 20-30 minutes on one page of your textbook, don't worry! That's normal and you must make sure you don't rush.

Rushing through too quickly is the most common mistake I see students make with their first layers. If you complete a 200 page textbook in a few days, alarm bells should start ringing. This usually indicates that you are not using the correct study technique (described in Chapter 8c) and skipping over difficult bits. This is the layer where it's ok to make mistakes and be a bit stubborn when it comes to understanding tricky concepts. To avoid rushing, within each topic, ask yourself "do I really understand this?" If not, break it down and take your time. It is at this point where time, to an extent, is on your hands.

Beth: *"How should I plan the second layer?"*

The layered learning timetable – layer two

If Beth executed her layer one as planned, she would then be ready to crack on with her second layer, approximately 10 weeks before her first exam.

Layer two			
Subject	Start date	End date	No. of days
Mathematics	7 March	11 March	5
English Language	12 March	16 March	5
English Literature	17 March	21 March	5
Science 1	22 March	26 March	5
Science 2	27 March	31 March	5
Science 3	1st April	5th April	5
Geography	6th April	10th April	5
German	11th April	15th April	5
ICT	16th April	18th April	3
Textiles	19th April	21 April	3

Beth: *"The second layer would be easier and quicker right?"*

Me: "Yes, but only if you executed the first layer thoroughly. With a few weeks left till exams start, your friends at school and teachers will start talking more about them. The pressure will be on and having completed your first layer you will be in a fantastic position."

Layer two – What you need to know

During this layer, it's important to cover one subject at a time. This is because exam timetables can sometimes be clustered and you may only have a few days in between to prepare for each exam. You may also have different exams falling on the same day. For example, a Physics exam in the morning and an English exam in the afternoon. The process of completing one subject at a time will train your mind to group the subject information together and pick it up quickly.

During layer one, it may have felt like you were taking a leap of faith. However, it is during this second layer that you will know for sure that the information is sticking. Working through each subject, you will start to notice that the material you learnt months ago which you thought you had forgotten was actually just sitting dormant in your mind. Everything will come rushing back and you will be able to work through topics at 2 to 3 times the speed you had done before. Nevertheless, confidence will be high so don't become complacent. Your momentum must be maintained!

Furthermore, start completing past papers after you finish each subject. Don't do all of them though – leave some for layer three.

Caution!
Having covered all required material once during the first layer, in layer two, you should not be covering or trying to understand concepts for the first time.

The layered learning timetable – layer three

With layer two done, the third layer will most likely be completed in the run up to exams and in the gaps between exams alongside past papers (past papers take priority though). Beth's second layer was scheduled to end on 21st April. However, in reality, unexpected setbacks like illness can and do occur so I added 7 days 'contingency time' before starting the third layer...

Sunday	Monday	Tuesday	Wednesday	Thursday	Friday	Saturday
	2nd Layer (L2) Complete	28 Physics L3	29 Physics L3	30 Physics L3	1-May Textiles L3	2 Textiles L3 ICT L3
3 ICT L3	4 Geography L3	5 Geography L3	6 Chemistry L3	7 Chemistry L3	8 Chemistry L3	9 Biology L3
10 Biology L3	11 Biology L3	12 Biology 1 + Biology 2	13 ICT 1	14 Chem 1 + Chem 2	15 English Lit L3	16 English Lit L3
17 English Lit L3	18 English Lit 1	19 Textiles + Geography 1	20 Physics1 + Physics 2	21 English Lit L3	22 English Lit 2	23 Maths L3
24 Maths L3	25 Biology L3	26 Geography L3	27 German L3	28 German L3	29 German L3	30 English Language L3
31 English Language L3	1-June English Language L3	2 English Language	3 German 1 + German 2	4 Geography 2 + Maths 1	5 Biology 1	6 Chemistry L3
7 Mathematics L3	8 Maths 2	9 Chem 3	10 Physics L3	11 Physics L3	12 Physics 3	13

L2 = Layer two
L3 = Layer three

Beth: *"I have 6 exams crammed in 3 days. How am I going to cope!?"*

Me: *"These exam clusters can be tricky. It's important to be strategic so that you don't struggle in the exams which don't give you much time to revise the morning before or night before..."*

How to handle exam clusters

To prepare for these exams in the middle of clusters, it's important that you complete the third layer for the last exam in advance. For example, take Beth's first cluster of exams on the 12th, 13th and 14th. Chemistry and ICT should be revised before Biology.

Sunday	Monday	Tuesday	Wednesday	Thursday	Friday	Saturday
	2nd Layer (L2) Complete	28 Physics L3	29 Physics L3	30 Physics L3	1-May Textiles L3	2 Textiles L3 ICT L3
3 ICT L3	4 Geography L3	5 Geography L3	6 Chemistry L3	7 Chemistry L3	8 Chemistry L3	9 Biology L3
10 Biology L3	11 Biology L3	12 Biology 1 + Biology 2	13 ICT 1	14 Chem 1 + Chem 2	15 English Lit L3	16 English Lit L3

To sufficiently prepare for the exams in the middle or end of the cluster (ICT and Chemistry in Beth's case), complete a quick 4th layer and work through past papers on the night before or of the morning of the exam. This extra layer will compensate for the lack of time you have before the exam.

Layer three – What you need to know

Layer three is crucial in gaining the most marks you can. It will ensure that information is fresh in your mind. Often students become tired at this point. However, I would urge you to remind yourself of why you are doing GCSEs in the first place. The end chapters within this book will help give you that push to continue.

At any point during your revision when you are struggling, remember the core point. In just x amount of days, I will be free to do as I please, with no associated feelings of guilt. I will sacrifice these days to reap a huge reward.

At this stage you should NOT be learning any new material. Your time is best spent re-reading the majority that you have learned well rather than trying to cram in a minority that you have not learned well. These days are used to re-familiarise yourself with the information that you already know, so that it is in the forefront of your mind ready to blast out with ease on the day of the exam.

I feel that layer three is really the 'make or break' round, but most importantly its effectiveness is dependent on the previous layers being completed. Try to skim-read through the topics and scribble down the key points from memory. Efficiently working through your learning material in this way, will help keep all the information to the forefront of your mind.

It's ok to become obsessed with doing layers!

Revising using layers, can make you quite an obsessive person. You will constantly feel paranoid about forgetting information and have the urge to squeeze in more layers. I used to randomly test myself and whenever I forgot a small piece of information, I would become extremely paranoid...Was this just the tip of the iceberg? How many other pieces of information have I forgotten?!

Having this paranoia pushed me to complete more layers particularly during the gaps between exams. On some difficult topics, I would complete up to six layers just out of fear that I'd forgotten everything. After six layers, there was no forgetting anything in those topics. I could have drawn out every damn picture on each page if you asked me to. The point is – the paranoia is good. Embrace it!

Beth: *"This all makes sense. I don't really see the point of going to school anymore!"*

Me: *"School is very useful. However, contrary to what everyone else thinks, it's much more beneficial to use your personal learning techniques as a primary tool and use your school/teachers/lessons as a secondary tool."*

Beth understood how the layered learning timetable was an effective way of planning revision in a way to maximise her chances of remembering information during exams. She followed through with my advice and went onto achieve 6A*s, 3As and a B (approximately six 8s/9s, three 7s and a 6). These grades helped her move to a better 6th form college to do A-levels and ultimately land a university place to study Medicine.

Feel free to use Beth's timetable as a template for your own. However, please remember that your plan doesn't have to be incredibly accurate. It's there to keep you organised, prevent you from feeling overwhelmed and therefore reduce your stress.

Beth's success story is one of many that have resulted from using this layered learning approach. However, it is only one piece of the puzzle. You also need to make sure you're learning the right stuff because let's face it – a timetable is pretty useless if you aren't!

In the next section, I'm going to show you how to pick your learning material. Doing so will ensure the time you invest executing the layered learning time table is not wasted and therefore give you the best possible chance of achieving 8s and 9s.

When to revise? Summary...

- Learning the same information again and again helps you remember more information for longer.

- The layered learning time table should be completed alongside all other school work.
- Layers summary...

Layer	Summary
1	• Cover one subject at a time or all together 'in tune' with school • Work through each subject thoroughly, making sure difficult parts are not skipped over • Use the correct study technique for each specific subject (described in chapter 9C)
2	• Spend approximately 5 days per subject • Cover one subject at a time • Work on past papers after completing each subject
3	• Spend 2-3 days per subject • Skim read or scribble down key points • Do not learn any new material • Complete <u>all</u> remaining past papers
4	• A quick 4th layer should be completed the night before the exam, particularly those which are in the middle or end of exam clusters

Chapter 8b: What to revise?

After constructing Beth's layered learning time table, she asked me to help her with some Maths homework that was due the next day. I agreed and we went to her room. After taking the micky out of the 'One Direction' poster on her door, I was shocked at what I saw. Piles and piles of hand written notes, revision guides, textbooks and school handouts.

Me: *"This is all a bit chaotic! What are you planning to revise from for each of your subjects?"*

Beth: *"Anything that my school gives me – I guess"*

Me: *"You have to be careful here. In the past I've spent hours working through summarised school handouts only to find out that they only covered 60% of the syllabus. Let's have a look at what you're planning to use for Biology..."*

Beth showed me a GCSE biology revision guide she bought from Amazon, an organised folder containing notes she took in class and a well-known website offering help with the subject.

Me: *"Were you planning on using all of these? Why did you choose these and not anything else?"*

Beth: *"Yes. A few of my friends recommended this revision guide and I quite like using the website because it makes studying Biology less boring."*

Me: *"Revision guides are beautiful. They are small, selective, colourful, filled with pretty pictures and promise to cover the entire GCSE curriculum in twenty pages...*

...They don't."

Revision guides: are they worth it?

Many revision guides try to filter the thicker exam-board text books into thin bullet pointed, diagrammatical and colourful pieces of text, but they miss out valuable bits of information which distinguishes a 9 and 4 grade student.

Remember that the core textbooks are written by the exam boards. They are written in the same language that you will need to use to answer the various exam questions.

In year 10, I remember comparing my boring looking thick biology text book with a thin colourful revision guide on the table and thinking "surely I don't need to read all that". I paid the price. While it may seem like a lot of hard work, it will be worth it.

Revision guides which are not designed for your specification, can be used as something to browse through in addition to your core textbook, but should never be used alone. They are an aid, not a substitute.

Beth: "I don't see what *the big deal is? Surely having more information and using different resources will help me memorise information easier and keeps things interesting – right?"*

Me: *"I have to disagree with you there. To achieve 8s and 9s at GCSE, you need to absorb all the <u>relevant</u> learning material but do this using the <u>least</u> amount of learning resources. You also have to pick these resources very carefully."*

Beth: *"I see...So what learning resources should I pick for each of my subjects? Can you show me?"*

Me: *"Sure..."*

How to pick your learning resources

Beth felt that having more information can't hurt and I sympathise with her because I used to have the same point of view. However, with the internet and all the other information out there, you risk going into information paralysis. To avoid this, I'm going to show you a procedure I've used time and time again to help choose the best learning resources.

Let's start by looking at the three most common learning resources available to you for GCSEs:

1. Text books
2. Handouts/slides or notes written during lessons
3. Revision guides (paperback and online)

First and foremost you have to verify your course textbook.

Verify your core textbook

For any given subject, the **core** textbook takes priority over every other type of learning resource. A core textbook is usually written by the same people who write your exams and they cover most if not all the information you need. However, these are not always available because exam boards constantly tamper with learning specifications. Therefore, a lot of the time, textbooks go out of date and your school then has to fill in the gaps within the textbook by producing their own learning material.

Nevertheless, if there is an up to date core textbook available, then your life becomes much easier and, depending on the type of subject, your chances of achieving a 9 sky rockets. So, how do you know whether your textbook is indeed a core up to do date version? Follow my procedure for each subject...

Step one: Find out what the exam board is. AQA? Edexcel? OCR? etc

Step two: Check the textbook itself:
  a. Does the textbook say it has been designed for your exam board?
  b. Check the date of publishing of your textbook (usually on the first 2-3 pages). Was it published less than 5 years ago?

Step three: Print out your learning specification from the exam board and compare it with your text book:
  a. Do the key learning outcomes in the specification match up with the heading and subheadings in the textbook?

If the answers to step two and three are yes then you probably have a core textbook. Things are looking good! However, you still need to double check with your teachers because it's their job to know the specification inside out and be aware of how relevant your textbook is.

Step four: Ask your teacher the following questions:
  a. Does this textbook cover the entire learning specification?
  b. If I learn this textbook front to back will I know enough to achieve 80% in the exam?

If the answers in step two to four are yes then it's time for a mini fist pump! This means your textbook is indeed a 'core' textbook, and is the only resource (alongside past papers) you need to achieve an 8 or 9. You can then go head and start your layered learning for this subject. This should be your bible right up till exams and, as long as you use my study techniques, you'll have a great chance of achieving a top grade. However, if steps one to four indicate that your textbook is out of date or not designed for your exam board, then a little more detective work needs to be done before you can start your layered learning timetable.

What to do if your textbook doesn't cover all the syllabus?

After showing Beth how to verify her textbooks, she followed steps one to four for each of her subjects. These were her results...

Subject	Is there an up-to-date core textbook?
Mathematics	Yes
English Language	Kind of
English Literature	No
Science 1	Yes
Science 2	Yes
Science 3	Yes
Geography	Kind of
German	No
ICT	Kind of
Textiles	Yes

Beth: *"With triple science, the textbooks were clearly custom made for my exam board. My teacher confirmed this too. So should I put my other science revision guides away and only use these?"*

Me: *"Yes. Going forward, whenever you sit at your desk to work on your layers in science, you should just have your textbook, a pen and a pad – nothing else."*

Beth: *"My maths teacher gave the OK for the text book. However, there's also an additional work book filled with practice questions available by the same authors/publishers. Should I use both?"*

Me: *"Yes."*

Beth: *"Geography and ICT both have textbooks that were published 4 years ago. However, there are parts of the specification which I didn't see in there. My teacher said the textbook is useful for some* *stuff but it's important to use the handouts/notes given in class as well."*

Me: *"It seems like the specification changed over the last 4 years. You'll need to piece together the required information using your specification. Do this...*

1. *Find your exam board specification online and print it out.*
2. *Take it with you to school and ask your teachers to show you which parts of the textbook are still relevant.*
3. *Stick a post-it note on the relevant chapters/pages.*
4. *Write down the textbook page numbers next to the learning outcomes in your printed specification.*

Remember that your textbook always takes priority so focus on these pages more when you work through your layers for ICT and Geography. Any learning outcomes in your specification which are not covered in the textbook should be covered during lessons and in your hand outs. So take your specification to class and make sure you make notes on anything not covered in the textbook. Also, to avoid loose pieces of paper, write these notes on your handouts."

Beth: *"I'm confused. For ICT and Geography, what resources should I revise from for my layers?"*

Me: *"When working on the layers you should have your printed specification, textbook with all the post-its, hand-outs and eventually your own additional notes after your teacher has finished the course on your desk. Make sure you tick off each learning outcome as you revise."*

Beth: *"OK. Got ya! For English, English lit and German my teachers said there are up-to-date textbooks available. However, they said sitting on my own and working through them will not get me a top grade."*

Me: *"I agree with your teachers. I admit that with the sciences and maths, although not advised, you can get away with dossing in class. However, to achieve top grades in languages, you need to be good at speaking and listening. Lessons are the only real place where you can practice."*

Beth: *"I should probably start paying attention then!"*

Me: *"Probably! So now that we have defined your learning resources for each subject, you can now execute your layered learning time table. Whenever you sit at home/library/school to work, your desk should have a pen, pad and your learning material – that's it"*

What to revise? Summary...

The procedure I used to help Beth pick her learning resources helped me to continuously achieve marks above 90% throughout my education. I encourage you to use it too!

By following the procedure, it will help you piece together your learning material and define exactly what you need to learn for exams. Doing so early in the year will put you in a fantastic position. While everyone starts panicking a few weeks before exams trying to find out what to revise, you'll have the answers and hopefully completed some layers too.

Summary flow chart: How to pick your learning resource?

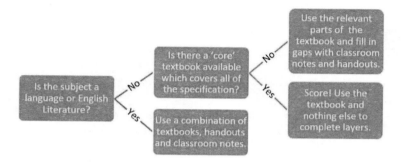

Chapter 8c: How to revise?

What are the key reasons why you may not have the required information in your head on exam day? Simple, you are either...

    # 1. Learning the wrong stuff

or

    # 2. Not learning enough of the right stuff

Be executing my advice in chapter 8b, you would have clearly defined what your learning material is and therefore have no problem with reason #1. However, what about #2? When you know what to revise, what is the best way to mentally store that information and ensure that you remember it.

In this section, I answer this question and dive into the topic of 'revision techniques'. Throughout my education, I've tried and tested many techniques. Most were absolutely useless but a handful worked really well and continue to help me to this day. I will show you these methods and describe how you can apply them to your individual subjects.

Memory technique...

Given that all your GCSE subjects are very different from each other, it would be logical to assume that you need to prepare for these exams in different ways. Would your preparation for a German written exam be different to a History exam? In many ways – yes. For example, your German exam may need you to string sentences together in the correct tense; for History you may need to write an essay on World War 2. Clearly, different skills are required, but what do they both have in common? Memorisation! Before answering any exam question for these subjects, you'll still need to memorise all the verbs and adjectives for German, and all the key facts about World War 2 for History. Regardless of how good your other skills are, if the required information is not in your head on exam day, you'll struggle to achieve top marks.

Memory techniques come before everything!

Me: *"Right. So Beth...You've finished school, come home, had dinner, sat down at your desk and opened page 1 of your physics textbook. Now what do you do?"*

Beth: *"Umm...Read through and learn it?"*

Me: *"How exactly? Let's get into details..."*

Beth: *"OK. I'd read over the first topic or section and try to understand it. Then write notes on that section"*

Me: *"What will you do with those notes after you're done?"*

Beth: *"I'd file them away in a folder and keep it organised so I can revise from them later"*

Me: *"I used to do that too. However, looking back, it was the reason why I performed so badly. Let me ask you something, given that you have a textbook that covers everything you need, is there any real point in taking notes?"*

Beth: *"Well yes. The textbook is so thick! Isn't it best to consolidate all the information into notes so I can revise from them later down the line?"*

Me: *"Unfortunately not. I know a lot of teachers and students suggest consolidating the textbook in this way, but it's probably the least efficient and most ineffective approach..."*

Note taking, is it worth it?

There was a time early on in my education, where I didn't really pay much attention to revision technique. During this period, I had built up certain assumptions about how I should revise and, similar to Beth, I adopted the idea that taking notes from my textbook or other learning material was an effective way to prepare for exams. I felt that reading through information, highlighting and summarising key points was a good learning method. I also thought reading over my notes closer to the exam would then seal the deal. Unfortunately, I was wrong and there are a number of reasons why...

1. Missing information and important details

Summarising the textbook into your own personal notes is a dangerous game to play, especially if you plan on using these notes to revise. Given that your exam boards could test you on practically anything from the course syllabus, how do you choose what to note down and what to leave out?

This is the way I see it. Let's say for example the textbook contains 100% of what you need to know. By summarising and cherry picking information that you felt was important, your notes would undoubtedly contain a fraction of the information in your textbook and therefore a fraction of the information required for your exam. For the sake of this example, let's assume this fraction is 70%.

200 Pages – 100% of Syllabus   50 Pages – 70% of Syllabus

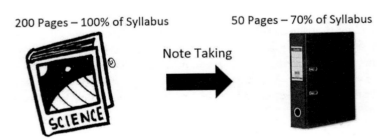

Note Taking

If you then use your summarised notes to revise, it will be difficult to retain more than 80% of the information in your notes. For arguments sake let's assume you do store 80% of the information from your notes in your memory. This means on exam day, your brain will contain 56% of the required course content (80% of 70% = 56%).

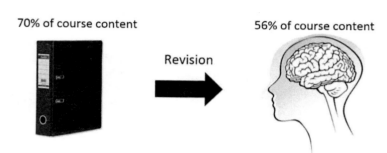

70% of course content

Revision

56% of course content

Coupled with the pressure and nervousness on the day, walking into the exam with only 56% of the required information does not give you a good chance of achieving an 8 or 9.

2. More likely to procrastinate & waste time

Do you ever go and get lots of coloured pens or little cue cards 'in preparation' to take notes?! What is the point of spending loads of time writing neat notes, or loads of illegible notes, with colourful diagrams, tip-exing all the mistakes when you can just read the textbook!?

I admit that the benefit of note taking, if done properly, is that you may find it easier to revise from your own notes, because they are in your own words. However, you have to ask yourself:

For the amount of extra time you have to spend preparing these notes, is it worth it?

3. Fool's gold

When taking notes it's easy to fool yourself into thinking you've done a lot of work when you haven't actually learnt much at all. I've met many students who feel copying out of a text book is a way of learning and also a valid way of completing a layer. I'm sorry to say, this is simply not true.

Don't get into the trap of studying just so that you can say that you did x hours of work today, to make yourself feel good or make your parents let you watch an extra hour of TV. Ask yourself what have you learnt? It's better to do one hour of revision and take 2 things in, rather than 5 hours and take in nothing!

Ace
Tips

Passive note taking is like writing on a typewriter without the keys making contact with the page – lots of effort and time spent but nothing retained.

In most cases the exam-board text books are presented in a clear and concise way, so there is no need to do any summarising or bullet pointing. <u>Learning directly from them is all that is required to achieve an 8 or 9</u>.

Beth: *"What if I re-word the information in textbooks and handouts in my own words."*

Me: *"It would be a better approach than just highlighting and copying. However, you'll still end up cherry picking all the important information."*

Beth: *"I have to admit – this does make sense. So if I shouldn't take notes, what should I do instead?"*

Me: *"You should learn <u>directly from your textbook</u> or other learning material using a method which I call 'The Scribble Technique'..."*

The Scribble Technique

This technique is a powerful memory tool that I've used time and time again. I attribute most of my exam success, particularly with those subjects which required a lot of fact learning, to this simple 8-step process...

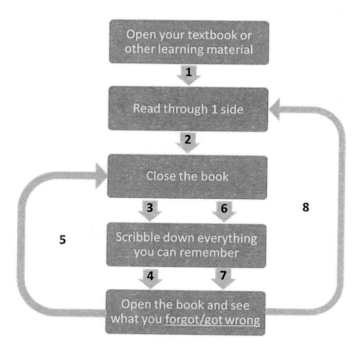

Scribble technique vs note taking: which is better?

The scribble technique on its own is a very effective way of absorbing information and holding facts in your memory for a long period of time. It's also a faster way of learning large volumes of information. The high efficiency and effectiveness of this technique makes it easier to bypass any note taking and focus on learning material there and then.

Using this technique for each layer can help you retain 80% if not more of the information in your text book.

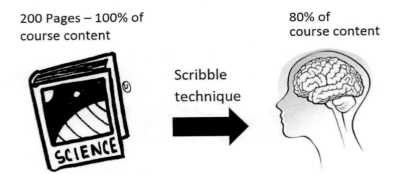

200 Pages – 100% of course content

Scribble technique

80% of course content

Focusing on memorising and learning the material, means you'll be happy to make mistakes and forget things when scribbling because you will open the page again and see what you got wrong or missed. The constant process of making mistakes and correcting them helps you retain information in a much faster and superior way to standard note taking.

To further explain, when you are trying to remember information to scribble down you will forget things. This will bother you in the same way it would if you forgot a song name that you wanted to download. When that song name pops into your head what do you experience? Probably a short pointless moment of joy! Chances are that song name will be nicely stuck in your memory from that point onwards.

Affective memory retention is all about creating those pointless moments of joy after challenging yourself to remember something. I know it just sounds silly, but you will realise its effectiveness if you try it.

If you don't remember the fact then that's fine because shortly you will find out, and instead of thinking *"Aha!"* you will say *"I knew it!"* It has a similar level of effectiveness but obviously the more you remember on your first go the better.

Scribble technique vs Candy Crush Saga

Although some of the information in your subjects can be interesting, it can be quite mind numbing to sit and work through the textbook. The scribble technique, at first, won't make the subject any more interesting for you. However, it will make the actual process of revision easier to bare. You may not understand this now, but if you start using the technique, it will very quickly turn into a memory game of 'how much can I remember this time round?' It's no 'Candy Crush' but it has just enough of the basic characteristics of a game to keep you interested. With practice, just as you become better at matching up candies in Candy Crush, you'll become better at remembering facts with the Scribble Technique. Just with any game that you play for long enough, you can also become addicted to it.

Beth: *"Addicted to revision? Are you joking?"*

Me: *"Dead serious. It's possible to become addicted to revision! If you don't believe me, try using the scribble technique for 3 consecutive days and see what happens!"*

Beth: *"OK. I'll try it but surely you're not suggesting actually memorising straight from textbooks?"*

Me: *"Believe me I know what you're thinking because I reacted the same way when I first heard about it. What changed my mind was finding out that everyone who learnt in this way were not only hitting A*s but high marks reaching above 90%. Those who made concise, neat, organised, time consuming notes and used summarised revision guides were usually in the B and C (5 & 4) range. It may be hard at first, but persevere."*

Beth: *"There is no way I can remember that much. Isn't that why we are told to take notes and summarise the key points in text books?"*

Me: *"You will be surprised how much you remember. I spontaneously did a biology past paper 2 months after using the scribble technique for my first layer and hit 62%. I can't put this down to luck as I got similar marks when I tried two more papers. Closer to the exam, after using the technique again for my second and third layers, I bumped up my final exam mark to 96%."*

Beth: *"I know people who are note takers and got A*s"*

Me: *"I'm not arguing that traditional note taking doesn't work, I'm saying that using the scribble technique with core text books works better because you learn directly using exam board information in a highly time efficient way."*

Beth: *"This is way too time consuming and I won't finish in time"*

Me: *"Overall time spent is actually lower when using the scribble technique because reading and scribbling takes less time than writing neatly. So the rate you cover material is higher (see appendix 1). On the first layer of my biology modules I could usually* *cover 10 – 12 A4 sides an hour. On the last layer, just before the exam, I could effectively cover 20+ sides an hour."*

Comparing the most popular learning methods

To summarise, I've compared the scribble technique with two of the most popular forms of revision.

1. Summarised revision guides – learning straight out of revision guides.
2. Note taking + later learning – taking notes from text books and using them to revise near exams.

The table below compares these two techniques with the scribble technique using three barometers.

- **Time:** looks at the estimated time you will spend working on any given subject.
- **Efficiency:** tests the volume of information you can *effectively* absorb per hour/day/week of studying.
- **Retention:** assesses the volume of information held in your memory and the length of time it stays there for.
- **Overall effectiveness:** The last row states the overall effectiveness of each method based on all the three barometers.

	Summarised Rev. Guide	Note Taking + revising from notes	Scribble Technique from Core Text book
Time	Low	High	Average-High
Efficiency	Good	Poor	Good
Retention	Poor	Average	Good
Overall Effectiveness	Low	Average	High

From this table, you can see that using the scribble technique overall is favoured and scores high in time, efficiency and retention. Everyone's different, and everyone works differently, but if your current method is failing you, I would advise you to give the scribble technique a try.

Beth: *"Should I use the scribble technique for all my subjects then?"*

What type of subjects have you taken and how do you revise for them?

For GCSEs I have split the subject types into three categories based on the way in which you need to answer exam questions. The most popular GCSE subjects have been categorised in the table.

Fact recall – The subjects that come under this category generally have large volumes of facts which you will need to memorise and recall in the exam. Exam questions would usually ask for <u>short answers</u>.

Method and understanding – These subjects require understanding, practice and a relatively small amount of fact learning. Exam questions would usually ask for <u>short answers</u>.

Written prose – Subjects that require the ability to convert facts and opinions into written prose. Exam questions would usually ask for <u>long answers</u>.

Subject	Fact recalling	Method and understanding	Written prose
Mathematics		•	
English			•
English Literature			•
Biology	•		
Chemistry	•	•	
Physics	•	•	
History	•		•
Geography	•		
Business Studies	•	•	
Religious Studies	•		
Design and Technology	•		
Physical Education	•		
Foreign Languages*	•		

*Foreign languages require learning words, using them in the correct tenses and stringing them into sentences. This requires practice.

As you see from the table, these categories can overlap. However, it is generally easy to distinguish between them. Each category requires a different approach when it comes to preparing for the final exam. For a subject like Physics, where you have an equal amount of fact-learning and method-understanding, a combination of techniques can be used. The section below will explain the optimum methods for each category based on my research and own experience.

Fact recall subjects

From the table, you can see the majority of GCSE subjects fall into the 'fact recall' category. In my experience, these subjects are the easiest ones to achieve 8s or 9s in. Why? Because exam questions rarely ask you to analyse information or to explain your opinion. Also, there is no room for interpretation because the answers to each question are clearly defined by the mark scheme. It's black or white. You either remember the facts and get the answer right or you forget and miss out on marks. The benefit is that you can focus all your efforts on memorising and nothing else.

How to revise on your own?

If your exam board textbook covers most of the syllabus, completing 3 layers and using the scribble technique is the surest way to achieve a 9. However, this is easier said than done because revising 'fact recall' subjects require a lot of mental discipline. You may need to learn large amounts of information that is comparatively more boring than other subjects. When students complain about not being able to focus with these subjects because it's boring, I always say 'Scribble first, take an interest later'. Let me explain...

I used to hate Biology and the other sciences. Never in a million years did I think I would develop a natural interest in these subjects. However, after using the scribble technique, something strange happened. I began thinking about the information I had learnt much more than I used to. At times daydreaming about it. Seeing a tree reminded me of photosynthesis. Babies reminded me of the reproductive process. What on earth was happening? Am I turning into a geek? Is this what is feels like to be a Nerd? Little did I know that I had developed an actual interest in Biology.

Did I broadcast my interest for Biology? Hell no. It was my secret!

What to do in class?

If your textbook and handouts cover everything you need for the exam, don't bother making any notes during class. Just focus on learning and understanding whatever is being taught. Teachers often pick up patterns in exams and can give hints on 'hot topics' that are likely to come up. Keep post-it notes ready and whenever your teacher drops a hint, stick one next to the relevant section in your textbook.

Furthermore, always look to learn information during class. If there's ever a quiet gap when the teacher isn't explaining something, scribble down the key points you remember from the information already covered in class.

Remember that, in addition to doing multiple layers, absorbing information through different channels improves the ability to retain content. These channels are reading, writing, speaking, hearing and doing. By being interactive in class you use all these channels at once and therefore improve your chances of remembering key information in the exam.

Method and understanding subjects

These subjects require calculation and mathematical problem solving.

How to revise on your own?

For method subjects like maths, the general advice that most teachers preach is practice, practice practice. I agree whole heartedly with this. Intelligence and a certain analytical mind can help with these subjects but this is by no means a prerequisite. The person who completes the most number of practice questions before the exam will usually get the higher mark – it's as simple as that.

Layered learning

During A-Levels, Maths mechanics was the first module I properly revised for after receiving my AS grades (I got a D). I was massively upset from my results and was feeling insecure and annoyed about not being 'smart enough' to do well. I felt like I had nothing to lose and wanted to prove a point to myself. I said to myself:

"If I do every single question in this Mechanics 1 text book and still don't get an A then it would truly prove I'm not cut out for this".

Over the remainder of the summer holidays I kept my word and completed every single question in that text book and worked through the answers. I used my classroom lessons as a strong second layer of the module and surprised both myself and my teacher with regard to how much I knew. That day I realised, I didn't get a D because I wasn't smart enough, it was because I wasn't practicing enough and revising properly.

As the exam period approached, and with 6 exams, I only had one day to recap my maths mechanics module. I was worried that I would forget all the content I'd spent my summer memorising, after all it was four months ago! However, the first 2 layers were strong and I was shocked when I hit 91% in the exam.

I realised that layering was the way forward, and while it seemed laborious, having cut out the time of making notes and faffing about in class, getting down to it and learning right from the start actually worked. From then I swore by the power of solid practice combined with layered learning.

Textbooks

Most textbooks provided by exam boards usually have answers to practice questions at the back of the book. If they don't it's important that you get them from your teachers. However, if you get stuck on a question it is critical that you don't look at the answer too quickly. Be stubborn and personally insulted by the fact you can't figure it out using your head; keep pounding at the question until you're exhausted. It's more beneficial if you come up with an answer and then check if it's right (even if your answer is wrong).

I remember occasions when I became extremely stubborn, refused to look at answers and minced at individual questions for long periods of time (sometimes more than an hour). This was very extreme and you don't need to do that but I thought it was worth emphasising.

In a similar way to the scribble technique described earlier, the process of pounding at a question and then having that 'light bulb moment' will create a strong memory. If that question comes up in the exam you will remind yourself and think 'this is that question which took me ages to figure out'. The more questions you do and the more stubborn you are with completing them without help, the better chance you are giving yourself of remembering what to do in the exam.

What to do in class?

With problem solving, there are always a bunch of tricks and short cuts which can make your life easier in the exam. Your teachers should show you these in class, so it would be a good idea to have a few sets of notes outlining all the important hints and tips. What you don't want is pages and pages of classroom notes with different examples explaining the same thing.

Written prose subjects

With 'written prose' exams, memorising information prior to your exam alone won't get you top marks. You need to be able to write essays coherently with the correct grammar and vocabulary. This is a different skill altogether and will therefore require preparation beyond the scribble technique.

How to revise on your own?

Preparation for these exams can best be described using the 'meal analogy'. To produce a meal, you need to gather the ingredients, cook it using the recipe and then present it nicely. Revising for a 'written prose' is analogous in the following way:

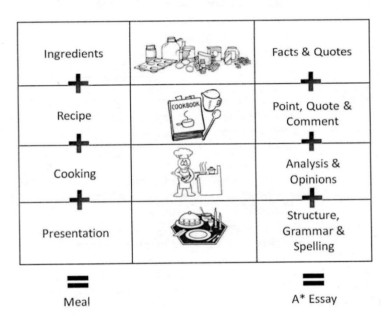

Ingredients **+**		Facts & Quotes **+**
Recipe **+**		Point, Quote & Comment **+**
Cooking **+**		Analysis & Opinions **+**
Presentation		Structure, Grammar & Spelling

| **=** | | **=** |
| Meal | | A* Essay |

Ingredients – Learning the facts

For subjects like History and RE, exams often ask you to use the 'source and your **knowledge**' to answer questions. The 'knowledge' part requires learning facts prior to the exam. As you probably guessed, the scribble technique can take care of this.

sh Literature, closed book exams now require memorising quotes. These can also be memorised prior to the exam in ne way.

Recipe – Point, Quote and Comment

You've probably heard a lot about 'Point, Quote and Comment' (PQC). However, if you haven't, PQC is the best method or recipe to use when answering exam questions for these subjects. The table below summarises what PQC is:

Key Area	What is it?	Example
Point	State a relevant point which helps directly answer the question.	Lenny was too innocent to comprehend loneliness.
Quote	Provide a quote or some evidence to back up your statement.	*"Tha's good,"* he said. *"You drink some, George. You take a good big drink."* He smiled happily.
Comment	Explain what the quote or evidence shows.	George has just reamed Lennie out for drinking too fast, but Lennie is so innocent that he doesn't even get mad. He just smiles 'happily' when George takes a drink. From this perspective, innocence doesn't look too bad.

It's important to practice using PQC. When interviewing students who've achieved A*s (8s/9s) in written prose subjects, like English Literature, many recommended using PQC and checking with teachers. This is a very useful iterative process because teachers can show how you can tweak answers to increase exam marks.

Cooking – Analysing and generating opinions

Before using PQC to answer exam questions, you'll need to analyse texts and generate opinions. This is particularly true in iGCSE/GCSE English Literature and English Language. Some people can read a passage or a poem and read between the lines quite effortlessly. I certainly could not and had to develop this skill over time.

For English Literature, knowing your text inside out is a huge help so make sure you read whichever texts your exam requires at least 5 times before sitting the paper. After you are familiar with the story and its characters, try and read between the lines. Ask why? Why did the author write this in the way he/she did? Why did the character say this? Why did this character react in the way they did? Write down what you think in the PQC format and show it to your teacher. Remember, the examiner is marking 1000s of papers, give your opinion or view. It doesn't matter if it's different to your teachers' interpretation.

You should however, also read through model answers and the marking specifications. It will give you ideas and help you form your own answers in the exam.

Presentation – Essay structure, spelling and grammar

Answers in your exams will need a structure. Be sure to spend 5 minutes jotting down an essay plan before answering each exam question.

What to do in class?

Written prose subjects are unique in that the exam marks are subjective to the marker. Experienced teachers often know what the examiners are looking for and can provide valuable advice during lessons.

For English and English literature, be a part of the conversation during lessons especially when analysing texts. These conversations will help you generate opinions during the exam.

Past Exam Questions and Mark Scheme

When it comes to past papers, I agree with the advice given by most school and teachers. The best way is to recreate exam conditions in your house, conduct the exam under a time limit, mark yourself harshly and correct what you get wrong.

Whenever students ask me how to get 8s or 9s at GCSE, my short answer is always use past papers. I put just as much emphasis on past papers as I do with core text books because:

1. They help calm nerves and fear of taking exams by imitating exam conditions. Nervousness can sometimes be a good thing giving you adrenaline, but most of the time it has a negative effect. Our minds don't work at full capacity when there is emotional churning going on. Most of the time we feel nervous because of uncertainty; not knowing what is going to come up and fear of not remembering content. My teachers used to say that if you complete past papers and mark yourself properly, the average mark of the last 3 papers is likely to be the result you get in the real exam. This rule of thumb held true for me and probably will for you. Therefore, you can pretty much predict what you're going to get in the exam before you sit it and reduce that debilitating uncertainty

2. Occasionally questions are changed slightly and repeated. Therefore, you can lock down those marks quickly and spend time on new questions

3. Completing all the available past papers essentially adds an extra layer before real exams

4. Studies done by Elevate Education show that top students do more past papers than anyone else. The founder of the company, Douglas Barton, made the following remark about the study:

"You can almost perfectly estimate a student's results by looking at the number of practice exams they've done. We also found that we could almost perfectly rank a class from first all the way down to last just given the amount of practice exams they would do across a year"

Predicting exam questions – the crystal ball approach

Many students compare past papers to try and pick out patterns and predict what questions will come up in the exam. Teachers usually recommend against this saying it's risky and difficult to predict anything because of how large syllabuses are. They are probably right but it still didn't stop me and many others from doing it. However, for any given module, it's more risky if you make predictions before properly completing 1 or 2 layers. This is because it will be easy to convince yourself that certain questions will come up and you'll probably end up selectively learning those parts while neglecting everything else. If you are going to take this crystal ball approach, then I recommend doing it late in the revision process and completing an extra quick rep of those topics you think will come up.

The mark schemes give you the structure of the answer they will expect of you in the exam. In a lot of subjects, students often miss marks not because of lack of knowledge, but because they did not know what the examiner is looking for. So, moral of the story – go through the mark scheme!

Mind mapping – mental filing system

Much of this chapter has explored the details of study technique. I would now like to take a step away from this and discuss the importance of keeping an eye on the bigger picture when it comes to learning the material for each module. What do I mean by this? It's very easy to become so bogged down in detail, that when it comes to exam questions, you struggle to recall the correct information or become mixed up with other things you have learnt.

You can tackle this by practicing past papers, but you also need to have an organised thought process so that you can pick out the correct pieces of information stored in your memory. Here's where things can go wrong. If you've focused on the details too much during your revision/layers, the organisation of that information in your mind may be poor. This can result in confusion during exams.

Let me give you an example...

In maths there are many methods that are similar; without proper mind mapping you can accidently use one method when you're supposed to use another. Integration and differentiation (from maths) are an example of such a scenario. These methods are used in calculus and using one instead of the other can result in completely the wrong answer.

Most people, including myself, create these mental mind-maps naturally while revising. However, I've come across some students who don't. Usually if a student with strong motivation and good revision technique underachieves, it's usually because of poor mind mapping.

Good vs poor mind mapping

The best way to gauge your mind mapping skills are to analyse how you link any given exam/practice question to the information required to answer it (in your memory bank). The diagrams below show the thought processes of a good and poor mind mapper:

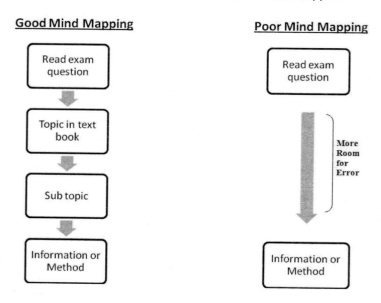

As you can see a good mind mapper not only learns the information or method, but also has an idea of what topic or chapter it falls under. Therefore, the topics are categorised and you can easily create clear dividing lines that leave less room for error and helps avoid mixing things up.

At first glance, the process diagram for 'Poor Mind Mapping' seems quite efficient. However, it leaves more room for error. With this method, you could end up recalling accurate information from the incorrect topic.

Are you a natural mind mapper?

You can identify if you are naturally good at mind mapping if you can bring up topic/chapter names during general conversation. For example, a Psychology student while discussing a module with his/her mates would probably ask questions like 'is that from chapter 4?' or 'didn't we cover that during that Cognitive Psychology lesson a few weeks back?' You can always tell when someone doesn't mind map because when you mention the names of certain topics or chapter headings, they usually have a blank look on their face.

If you don't naturally mind map, what can you do?

After the first layer of a subject, I could usually think of a piece of information, open up my textbook and pick out the chapter it was in. In some cases I could remember the actual page. You might be thinking... surely that is difficult to do? The answer is no – not if you adopt certain habits during your study cycle. These habits are regularly reviewing material, reaffirming topics and physical mind mapping.

Regularly reviewing previous material
Every time you finish a study session in your mind, briefly go over the information you have covered, summarise it into a few lines and remind yourself of the topic and/or subtopic it falls under. Repeat this on a day-to-day basis when you sit down and start to study for the same module again. This shouldn't take more than a couple of minutes.

Reaffirming topics
Be the person who knows all the names to the chapters and topics. Talk about the chapters out loud when discussing with friends or teachers to reaffirm them. When you're in lessons and the teacher brings up a topic, think about the summaries you have made during self-study. You'll surprise yourself at how much it helps.

Physical mind mapping

Physically drawing out mind maps can be very beneficial. If you haven't come across them before, here's an example of one for Physics.

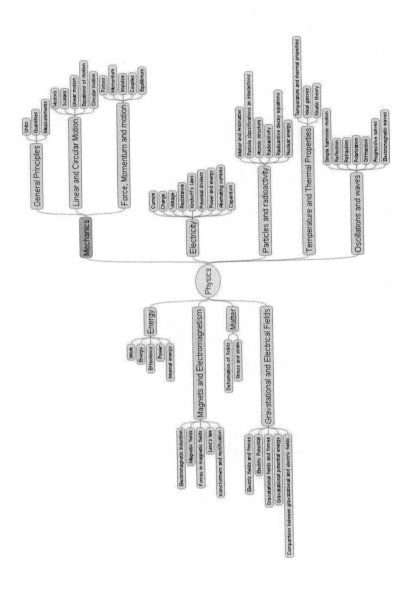

79

Before the actual exam use the mind map as a guide and run through in your mind the topics and summarisations you've made for them.

Mind Mapping Tutorial

There are also some apps and websites that can help you build mind maps. However, I recommend doing it the old fashioned way and drawing them out on an A4 or A3 piece of paper.

Step 1: Write your module name at the centre of the page.

Step 2: Choose the labels for the first layer of branches. If you have a good exam textbook then it's best to use the chapter headings.

Step 3: Draw out branches to key topics under each chapter.

Given that we want the mind map to show an overview of a subject or module, I wouldn't produce any further branches. As you read over your mind map think through, or jot down on a piece of paper, the important details that fall under each topic.

In my own experience I never consciously or physically made a mind map. However, by thoroughly reviewing modules and spending large amounts of time on chapters/topics, I naturally made my own mental filing system. If you find that you are unable to do this, you must make a conscious effort to do so. Take time out from your study cycle and physically write out mind maps.

This skill will become massively beneficial during A-levels as information from different modules (not topics) can overlap. Effective mind mapping will save a significant amount of time.

Bag of tricks...alternative memory techniques

For some exam questions you occasionally have to memorise information in the form of an item list or a process. For example, in biology, transcription is a process whereby a protein molecule is built in a cell. This process has 6 steps which students will need to remember for the exam. Usually layered learning and the scribble technique are powerful enough to commit this information to memory, however it doesn't hurt to have a few more tricks up your sleeve. This is to really make sure you remember all you need in the exam.

Our minds can only remember a limited number of items at a time. Even after layers, some information is awkward and arduous to memorise. Picture association and Mnemonics are useful aids for these scenarios. Let's have a look at them...

Picture association

This technique involves creating memory triggers by first associating objects with numbers and then the objects with information we want to learn. Our minds find it easier to remember objects and scenarios as opposed to numbers or facts. Therefore, we can use an object to create a mental link between the items of information we want to learn and the corresponding item number.

This technique is not only useful for an item list which has to be remembered in a consecutive order, but also if you need to call upon a specific item or number.

For example, earlier I mentioned the transcription process most biology students need to learn. In step 2 of the transcription

cess, an enzyme called RNA polymerase unwinds and unlinks
the two strands of DNA. In the exam you may have to recall this
specific step or know where this step occurs in the process. With
picture association you can easily remember the object associated
with the step no. and therefore remember the information
associated with the object.

Picture association tutorial:

Step 1: Assign memorable objects to numbers 1 – 15. Use the ones
we have here.

Number	Object	Reason
1	Tree	1 tree stands alone
2	Light Switch	2 options: on and off
3	Traffic Light	3 options: green, amber and red
4	Dog	A dog has 4 legs
5	Glove	A glove has 5 fingers
6	Devil	The devil's number is 666
7	Heaven	7 rhymes with heaven
8	Skate	8 rhymes with skate
9	Cat	A cat has 9 lives
10	Bowling Ball	10 pin bowling
11	Twin Towers	September 11th attacks and the twin towers looked like 11
12	Eggs	12 Dozen in a pack of eggs
13	Pumpkin	13 is "unlucky" – Halloween – pumpkin
14	Flowers	14th Feb is Valentine's day where you give/receive flowers
15	Cinema Ticket	Only over 15's allowed for some cinema movies

Once you have memorised and associated each number to an object, these objects become **Number Associated Objects**.

This means the number and object are interchangeable – whenever you think of no. 2 you should almost immediately think 'light switch' and vice versa.

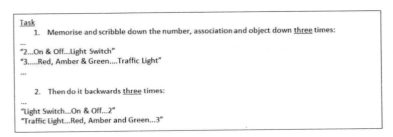

Task
1. Memorise and scribble down the number, association and object down <u>three</u> times:

...
"2...On & Off...Light Switch"
"3.....Red, Amber & Green....Traffic Light"
...

2. Then do it backwards <u>three</u> times:

...
"Light Switch...On & Off...2"
"Traffic Light...Red, Amber and Green...3"

Step 2: Use your imagination to link the **Number Associated Object** to the item of information. You do this by playing out a memorable scenario using your imagination.

For example, for step <u>2</u> in the transcription process, we can imagine the <u>RNA polymerase</u> approaching the DNA strand and pressing a <u>light switch</u> which then causes the <u>DNA to unwind</u>.

This method might sound quite silly but that's exactly why it will stick in your head. It's easier for your mind to remember scenarios than sentences/numbers and it's even easier if those scenarios are funny or crazy.

Note: When imagining the scenario, close your eyes and make it very vivid and clear. This will help the scenario stick in your memory.

Mnemonic

This is a common technique backed by many studies, used to help retain and recall information. In this section we will explain the two most effective types of mnemonics: music and expression or word.

Music

Are you one of those people who can recite song lyrics after only hearing it a handful of times? I personally am not. However, if you are it's probably because the fundamental systems in your mind are highly sensitive to melody and beat. This can be useful for remembering information.

When I mentioned music mnemonics you probably thought of the 'ABC' song used to help primary school kids learn the alphabet. However, although useful, this is not the technique I am referring to. Instead of creating song lyrics out of information, a more efficient way to use your 'musical mind' is to use songs in conjunction with the scribble technique. This can be done by reading (out loud or in your mind) information from your text book in a song like way or like a jingle. You can then benefit from combining the highly efficient forgetting-remembering cycle in the scribble technique with the mental links created using your unique 'musical mind'.

Expression or word

Using expression or word mnemonics is also a useful memory technique. When memorising a list of items you can produce a word mnemonic using the first letter of each item of information.

For example in English, to join two clauses together you use coordinating conjunctions. These are for, and, nor, but, or, yet and so. These can be remembered using the word mnemonic FANBOYS. An expression mnemonic can also be used...

For	And	Nor	But	Or	Yet	
Four	Apples	Nearly	Broke	On	Your	Sidew

If you don't want to spend time thinking of mnemonics like these then you can find existing ones online or by using mnemonic calculators.

In comparison to the scribble technique, in my opinion both these techniques are less efficient. Therefore, I would only use them for memorising a large number of concepts or for information that you are struggling to retain even after several layers. Please do not replace the scribble technique with these alternative memory tricks – you will probably run out of time!

How to revise? Summary...

- Taylor your revision to the type of subject: Fact recall, Method & Understanding or Written prose.
  - o Fact Recall – Using the scribble technique with your core textbooks is the best way to memorise information for your exams.
  - o Method & Understanding – The more practice questions you do the more chance you have of achieving a top grade.
  - o Written prose – The scribble technique will help you memorise facts and quotes. However, essay practice is equally if not more important.
- Always complete exam questions under timed and exam simulated conditions.
- Use mind maps to help organise your subject information.
- Mnemonics and picture association are additional tools you can use to help learn awkward information.

Step 1: Method - summary

From layered learning, to picking your learning resources, to the scribble technique and everything in between, the first step of the 3 step plan is crucial to achieving 8s and 9s. The details are important, but it's important to understand the bigger picture:

Revision isn't some casual learning process. It should be more industrial. Your study room at home should feel like a factory where every time you sit down to work, the factory turns on and information starts being processed and stored in your brain. It's your job to design the factory in an efficient way and equip it with the right tools so that the process of learning is done quickly and effectively.

By reading through this chapter, you have equipped your factory with the best tools in the business – so use them!

Chapter 9: Step 2 - Study Cycle...Am I Working Hard Enough?

The 'study cycle' is the day-to-day routine you go through as a GCSE student. Having a productive cycle or routine is important. After all, what is the point of knowing all these great study techniques if you can't sit yourself down and get some work done when you need to!

Eat, sleep, study, repeat!...

What makes the study cycle tick? The conversations you have with yourself day-to-day. I'll compare 3 students to show you how much these conversations matter and the consequences of not managing them and your time properly.

There's work to be done...

After reading about the layered learning timetable, it's probably quite clear that you need to make some sort of sacrifice. I could have lied to you and given you a magic 20 day plan; promising you 8s and 9s with no work. However, it wouldn't have been true. There is work to be done, but how can you tell if you are doing enough to achieve a top mark in your exams? We don't have any crystal balls so we have to determine what 'enough' is. To help you do this, I introduce you to a student who achieved top grades after practically failing all of his year 10 modules and mocks. We compare his typical day (before) when he _thought_ he was working hard and (after) when he _actually_ was working hard.

Influences...

Most of this chapter will demonstrate how the conversations you have with yourself are important. You don't need to walk too far to realise that your environment and the conversations you have with others also have an impact. Your friends, family and idols all shape your beliefs. It's those who you are closest to who sometimes determine whether your study cycle runs like a smooth Ferrari or a banged up Skoda.

Staying on track...

When you are knee deep in the layered learning time table, how do you know if you're on track? I show you how to measure your productivity.

Staying productive...

Study leave is an intense period of time. When the pressure is on, I show you some tricks that can help you stay productive.

What is the 'Study Cycle'?

The study cycle is the process you participate in on a day-to-day basis during your academic life. It has three elements which are intent, action and maintenance.

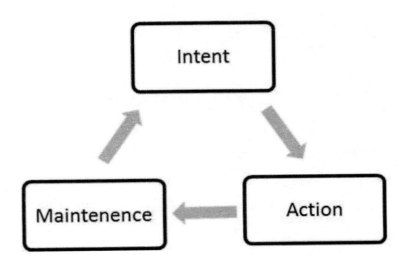

Intent – How often you think about or feel like working?

Action – How often do you act on your intent and start working?

Maintenance – How effectively, and for what length of time do you work for, before needing a break?

We asked three different students (James, Rajesh and William), all with varying GCSE results, about their study cycle and how effective they are at executing each of the three elements. Read the 3 profiles on the next page and see if you can relate to any of them.

	James – A*/A	Rajesh – B/C	William – D/E
Intent	Usually on the way home from school, I think about what I need to get done. I generally think about my study schedule a lot.	School is tiring so all I usually think about on the way home is TV. I do think about studying a lot when there is pressure say from a strict teacher or if there's a mock coming up.	I do think about studying, but only when I'm not thinking about or doing other things like watching footy or chilling with friends. However, I do want to do well in my exams.
Action	Sitting down and starting revision is usually the hardest part for me. However, I hate that feeling of guilt when I don't get anything done. Usually thinking about that guilt gets me to go up to my room and get stuck in.	When there is no immediate pressure, my parents force me to work more then I force myself. There just seems to be far more interesting things to see and do than study.	On Saturday my dad usually wakes me up at midday and reminds me to do my work. I have a tendency to put studying off so I lie in bed for ages and then go for a long shower. This carries on till the evening and then I get tired and think 'it's getting late now – I'll just do it tomorrow'. But the same thing happens again on Sunday!
Maintenance	After starting a study session, I can usually build momentum. Yes, I do procrastinate and start looking at my phone, but I hate leaving things unfinished. Thinking about how I'm going to relax after I finish helps me push on.	On those occasions I do get started, I'm actually not that bad and get work done. After, I often ask myself what's the big deal? Why can't I just do this every day and avoid getting in trouble at school or with my parents.	I know studying will help my future etc. but I just don't find any of it interesting. Also, I find it all a bit too daunting at times and when I think about all the work I need to do, I just become negative and give up.

90

Of course there are many more variations than the examples in the table, but it will give you a good idea of the differences in thought processes. You have to be effective in all three study cycle elements across days, weeks and months to become a high performer.

All three students were aiming for high grades and felt they were working hard enough to achieve them. So why were their final grades so different? The answer lies in their perception of 'hard work' and the assumptions they made to shape that perception.

What is hard work?

"I worked really hard for my exams and I still only scraped Cs"
-Ali

Hard work is a common phrase. Have you ever thought about what hard work actually is? You probably hear it all over the place like during assembly, from your teachers and parents. But what *exactly* is working hard? It's a phrase that is thrown around so much by everyone with very little explanation. I believe that working hard is a skill in itself and the lack of detail or definitions on this is one of the main reasons why students misjudge what they need to do to get high marks.

Unfortunately, once upon a time, I also made the same misjudgement and many others also do. This is why I went on a mission to find out what high performers like James were doing in their free time. I tried to find out everything about their habits, routines and perception of hard work.

He's always with mates or playing footy, but yet he gets an A*

At school it was tough to balance my social life and my work life. Firstly, I had my parents on my case about staying in and revising. Then, I had my friends constantly asking me to go out. It was hard to find a balance. I obviously wanted to go out, it's tough to stay in and work when your mates are playing football or at the cinema. However, I used to think if they could do it and get straight As, then so could I; that's where I was wrong. Out of that group of friends 4 were in the C/D (4s/3s) range or under; 3 got Bs/Cs (5s/4s) and 3 got As/A*s (7s/8s/9s).

When interviewing my 3 friends who achieved As/A*s, I asked about their study habits and compared them with my own. What was most frustrating was that I wouldn't consider myself to be less intelligent in comparison to them. In actual fact I'd say we all had pretty similar intelligence. I soon found out that the difference was how we managed our time.

Looking back it seems quite obvious; you see, after school, I'd get home and have about 3 or 4 hours where I'd watch TV, eat my dinner, do maybe an hour of homework, have a shower and then get ready to go out. This was where my friends and I differed.

I expected them to all be crazy undercover workaholics – they weren't. It seemed most of them just worked for a couple of hours every day. My friend Tom said:

"I just thought to myself, I really need to concentrate and learn the next three chapters so then I can go out and have fun."

Their remarks got me thinking about my own habits and how I could change them to help achieve what they did.

After some thought, I realised that my study cycle was bad because I was unaware of how much and how often I needed to work. My ignorance resulted from having certain assumptions that I didn't question. However, once I realised where I was going wrong, I was able to improve my day-to-day habits.

Thinking independently and making small adjustments in attitude helped me become proactive during certain periods of the day. The most significant improvement happened once I changed my habits at home.

Everyone tells you to work hard but most people don't understand what working hard entails. You may think coming home after school, doing your homework and watching TV most of the year is sufficient to get the grade you want. Or that reading over your notes on the train, spending an hour at home doing text-book exercises and taking the weekend off is sufficient. Unfortunately it's not.

So what is a good routine?

The best way to answer this question is by showing you an example. Steve was one of many students I've mentored, but I've chosen him as an example because he had no idea that his routine was bad until I intervened. He was oblivious as he was known for being the 'studious one' among his friends and family. Even though his grades didn't warrant any praise, his friends kept saying things like "If I only had the motivation Steve has" and "wassup Einstein". Hearing these remarks made him believe in his own reputation and was convinced into thinking he was on track for A*s and As.

From the first time I met him in year 10, I noticed his delusion. Even though I tried to make him aware of this, he kind of just shrugged off my opinion and said

"Ye. Ye. I see what you mean. So what do you think I should take for my A-levels?"

After failing his year 10 mocks and module exams, I thought his results would help him wake up. It didn't! Everyone kept fuelling his delusion by telling him he "tried his best" and "deserved better". Enough was enough. I staged an intervention at his house with all his family. Only after explaining my thoughts did his view start to change. Over time his entire study cycle improved and his grades did too.

After receiving GCSE results of 7A*s, 2As and 2Bs, I asked Steve to compare his typical daily routine during year 10 and year 11. From the point he woke up to the moment he went to sleep, this is what he wrote...

	Typical Day – Year 10 Result: Cs & Ds	Typical Day – Year 11 Result: A*s, As & Bs
Early Morning	I'm up out of bed, walk to school and try to get in on time to avoid detention. While walking, I usually stress about the homework I didn't do on the previous day and frantically try and brain storm excuses to tell my teachers. During morning registration, more often than not, I borrow completed homework from my friends which I copy.	Soon after waking up, I run through what I need to get done by the end of the day. I then put on some music and walk to school or catch up with friends if I meet them on the way. During morning registration, others usually approach me to copy my homework. It's actually quite annoying because I put the effort in. Why should I share it?
Lessons	I usually try to concentrate during lessons and am not afraid to put my hand up to ask or answer questions. However, I get into trouble because my homework is usually rushed or unfinished.	The time and energy saved worrying about what excuse I'm going to tell the teacher is now better spent on actually listening in class. This GCSE stuff isn't actually that difficult to understand.
Breaks	When the lesson's over, I'm gunning for the door to go play footy or catch up with mates.	Play footy or catch up with mates. However, often I'd stay back 5 minutes if I need to ask the teacher a question.
After School	I head down to the shops with mates or go home if I'm tired.	I now hate faffing around after school so I head home, I've got better things to do then stand outside a chip shop putting my mates in headlocks.
Home	Usually I get home at 16:30, sit on the sofa and turn the on the telly. I keep my homework next to me so I can work on it during the adverts. If I don't finish my work it's fine because I can wake up early to do it or copy off someone.	The moment I get home, I go upstairs to my room, write down a to-do list and open my textbook. Even though I don't start right away, this sets the 'theme' for the evening. After having dinner, I properly get started usually around 5pm and push through till 8 or 9pm. Then I relax by playing PS3 with mates online or watching telly with my family.

By comparing both days it's clear that in certain parts of the day some changes were more drastic than others. Steve and I discussed the comparisons he made...

Me: *"You made a lot of positive changes between year 10 and 11. What was the most significant one?"*

Steve: *"Not switching on the TV as soon as I got home. It was a habit so it took a while to break out of it. When I finally did, it seemed to trigger a domino effect. Everything else became easier. Writing a to-do list and starting my layers instead of watching TV meant I could finish earlier, relax and have no problem with teachers the next day. It's so surprising how simple changes like that can make a difference."*

Me: *"How did you break that habit of watching TV immediately?"*

Steve: *"It was more difficult than I thought it would be. I was actually addicted to TV. I think I had withdrawal symptoms after cutting down! One day I just said to myself 'right – don't even look at the TV. Just run straight upstairs and get started'. After doing this a few days in a row, I cut my TV watching down in the same way a smoker cuts down on cigarettes. Just how addiction to cigarettes are harmful on your health; addiction to TV, facebook, twitter etc are harmful to your grades."*

Me: *"How did you organise your time at home?"*

Steve: *"As you know, I used the layered learning timetable. Each day I would have a set target. For example, I would set myself a goal of completing the scribble technique on 10 pages of my science textbook. This would take me about an hour and a half to complete. After that, I'd just finish off any homework or work on coursework. Even just getting a few pages completed each day adds up over time. I was absorbing everything properly so I knew that completing the first layer for a subject was pretty much a guaranteed A*."*

Me: *"Did you do this every day?"*

Steve: *"No. I used to play for a local football club so I had practice once a week. Occasionally I would come home too tired and found it hard to concentrate so I would go out and meet friends. My schedule was all over the place sometimes but across weeks and months, the overall affect was positive and a lot more was getting done in the right way."*

Me: *"What else changed between those 2 years?"*

Steve: *"My entire attitude really. In year 10 I was convinced that everything would turn out ok in the end as long as I went to school every day. I was complacent and coasting through if you like. However, after flopping my mocks and speaking with you, reality hit. All of a sudden, I looked at my calendar and felt very short of time. With around 20 exams in year 11, it was clear my entire routine needed to change and fortunately it did."*

Me: *"Did you think about studying more often?"*

Steve: *"In year 10 hardly, but in year 11 all of the time. I found myself feeling guilty a lot when I wasn't studying"*

Me: *"It seems like the guilt was a good sign. It told you what your priorities were"*

Steve: *"Ye I agree. For me feeling a small amount of guilt all the time was normal. In fact it was necessary because it pushed me to get on with what I had to do even when I was tired"*

Me: *"You said that others started asking you to copy your homework instead of the other way round. So did you turn into the class geek?"*

Steve: *"HaHa. Not quite! I found it quite annoying when others asked me and I couldn't believe that only a year ago, I used to be the one asking all the time. I did occasionally let people copy if I felt sorry for them."*

Me: *"Did your approach to class change?"*

Steve: *"Yes a lot. With so many exams, I needed to make the most of my time so I treated each class as a layer. Most of the time I'd just try to understand what my teachers were explaining. The way I saw it was – the more I understood in class the less I'd have to figure out on my own at home."*

Me: *"After all of this – was it worth the hard work?"*

Steve: *"Definitely. I'm so glad I made the changes I did to my routine. My grades bought me a lot of respect from my family and surprisingly my friends too. Also, I recently received an offer to study medicine at Birmingham university. They only really give places out to students with 5A*s at GCSE. I couldn't have got in without the grades I achieved."*

Steve was no natural genius. In fact, as part of my research, I got him to do an IQ test and the results were average. Intelligence had nothing to do with his success. Questioning his assumptions and truly understanding what an A* student does on a daily basis, were the key factors here. The change in his attitude improved every element of his study cycle, and after kicking his bad habits, he started working on 'auto-pilot'. Studying became effortless and second nature to him.

Reading Steve's story might leave you asking: How did Steve get over his delusion? How did you get him to question his assumptions and convince him that his assumptions were wrong? I did this by explaining how his assumptions about learning and hard work were shaped by the influences in his life and environment.

Influences

My mum used to constantly talk about 'bad influences'. She used to say "Your friends are a bad influence on you!"

Those around you shape your assumptions. Your mates in particular have a large part-to-play in what you believe to be true. From my research and experience, students gauge how often or how much they need to work by what their mates are doing. Most of us are naturally inclined to go along with the crowd rather than think independently. In other words, it's easy to assume that what you are doing is ok because everyone else is doing it.

Friends...

The influence of your friends can be so subtle that you don't even notice that it's happening. For example, on a number of occasions I heard my mates say "Don't worry! We can always retake next year". This phrase was etched in my mind and I often re-affirmed it to myself as an excuse to procrastinate. This turned into an assumption that didn't budge because I never chose to question it. It was true, I could re-take the module if it went sour. However, I should have been thinking what would happen if I messed up a bunch of modules? Then I'd have loads more exams in the next term and have less time to spend on each one. I shouldn't have continued to reaffirm the damaging assumption.

Whenever you think you've made a wrong assumption, tackle it early. Write it down, question and consider the consequences of it.

Further evidence of peer influence can be seen by simply observing friend circles. In my school, some groups were known for always doing well and some were known as the 'dossers'. It was clear that the 'dossers' were feeding each other wrong assumptions and constantly reaffirming them. As a result they all underperformed together. However, the opposite occurred within those friend circles that were known to do well. They seemed to directly and indirectly push each other forward through healthy competition. In my experience working with like-minded people can propel you even further. This became apparent to me during university where I was one of four graduates who achieved first class honours and given a Deans List certificates for academic excellence. The other three were my best mates – this was no coincidence. I'm not saying go and make friends with the geekiest group in your year group, but try and encourage your friends to study with you. It helps knowing some-one else out there is going through the same deal as you.

Family...

It's important to also be aware of the influence of your environment. Early on in my education, my assumptions had built gradually over time from years of seeing my parents watch TV for hours after work, mates jumping on Facebook and Twitter as soon as they got home. As a result, I always assumed that everyone else was doing the same thing.

When I asked my cousin, who got all A's and is now a doctor, about what he did in the evenings and on weekends I was quite shocked. Not surprisingly his parents worked till late and would encourage him to make the most of those hours. If you are a reactive person and no one physically tells you about other people's habits, then you will assume your study cycle and work ethic is fine. Furthermore, you probably won't go asking about others habits until you realise something is wrong i.e. achieving bad grades.

Smart phones...

Question. What contains a bunch of distractions and follows you around everywhere? You guessed it – your smart phone. With all the games, instant messaging and social media apps, becoming addicted to your phone is not difficult. Above all, the instant messaging apps like WhatsApp prove to be the top distractions.

This is because smart phones have made us feel uncomfortable when there is information on the phone that we have not seen yet. Let me ask you, do you get uncomfortable about having the little star or the 'unread' symbol on the top right of your Facebook, Twitter or WhatsApp icons? Or un-watched stories on Snapchat?

If you find it hard not to click on unread posts/messages/tweets or stories, then you're addicted to social information. You're not alone! Addiction to technology is on the rise and there's a reason for this.

What do you think makes more money than movies, game parks and sports combined? Slot machines. How can slot machines make all this money when they are played with such small amounts of money? They are played with coins. How is this possible? Well, your phone is pretty much an advanced version of a slot machine. Every time you check your phone, you're playing the slot machine to see, what going to appear? Every time you pull down or scroll a news feed, you're playing to see what information you're going to get next. Our obsession with technology is not an accident.

Mobile technology development companies have invested billions of pounds into creating apps that keep us hooked. Some are even hiring PHDs specialising in human psychology and addiction. At the time of this writing, Pokemon Go has been downloaded 100 million times and makes over £1 million a day. Seven out of ten users who download the app, return to it the next day and spend on average forty minutes a day playing the game. Now, do you really think it's possible to study with your phone nearby?

With such a sophisticated piece of technology, you are asking too much of your will power. As your concentration fades during study periods, you become more susceptible to procrastination and seeing the blinking light or push notification on your phone is all it takes to break your concentration. Do yourself a favour. Switch your phone off before you start working and hand it to your mum or dad. Out of sight – out of mind. Doing this alone will probably improve your exam marks by 10% minimum!

Measuring your Hard Work

How do you measure how hard you are working?

It's simple, you have to gauge whether you are being productive, not productive compared to your friends. You have to be productive to your own standards, only you know your boundaries, push them! Find out when you work the hardest, how do you know when you've really worked hard? I have friends who say they know they've worked hard because they 'forgot to eat' others have said that they get so tired they need naps between revision. Find out what works for you.

Furthermore, take a step back every two weeks and check how much you've accomplished. It's important to be precise and to use a marker to calculate your work rate. For example, I used the number of text book pages I covered per week to track my progress. When you calculate your work rate ask yourself: Am I doing enough to hit my target or complete my layer by the date I've set? If the answer is no, make further use your free time, particularly on evenings and weekends to boost your work rate.

How to revise on your own?

Preparation for these exams can best be described using the 'meal analogy'. To produce a meal, you need to gather the ingredients, cook it using the recipe and then present it nicely. Revising for a 'written prose' is analogous in the following way:

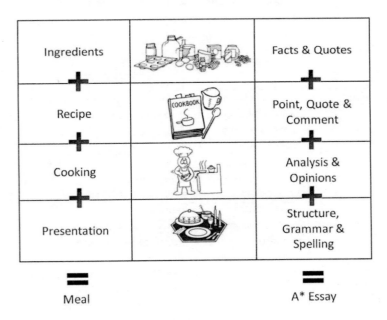

Ingredients **+**		Facts & Quotes **+**
Recipe **+**		Point, Quote & Comment **+**
Cooking **+**		Analysis & Opinions **+**
Presentation		Structure, Grammar & Spelling

=		**=**
Meal		A* Essay

Ingredients – Learning the facts

For subjects like History and RE, exams often ask you to use the 'source and your **knowledge**' to answer questions. The 'knowledge' part requires learning facts prior to the exam. As you probably guessed, the scribble technique can take care of this.

For English Literature, closed book exams now require memorising the key quotes. These can also be memorised prior to the exam in the same way.

Recipe – Point, Quote and Comment

You've probably heard a lot about 'Point, Quote and Comment' (PQC). However, if you haven't, PQC is the best method or recipe to use when answering exam questions for these subjects. The table below summarises what PQC is:

Key Area	What is it?	Example
Point	State a relevant point which helps directly answer the question.	Lenny was too innocent to comprehend loneliness.
Quote	Provide a quote or some evidence to back up your statement.	*"Tha's good,"* he said. *"You drink some, George. You take a good big drink."* He smiled happily.
Comment	Explain what the quote or evidence shows.	George has just reamed Lennie out for drinking too fast, but Lennie is so innocent that he doesn't even get mad. He just smiles 'happily' when George takes a drink. From this perspective, innocence doesn't look too bad.

It's important to practice using PQC. When interviewing students who've achieved A*s (8s/9s) in written prose subjects, like English Literature, many recommended using PQC and checking with teachers. This is a very useful iterative process because teachers can show how you can tweak answers to increase exam marks.

Don't leave any room for regret...

You do not want to be one of these people who will regret these 2 years for the rest of your life, knowing that you can do better. It is time for you to be serious and look out for yourself. Yes, your social life does matter. I'm not trying to scare you, but not making your work a priority can permanently damage your future. Once you leave school, there will be a very small number of people who you will keep in touch with. The rest will disappear into the deep depths of your Facebook contacts – you know, the ones that never appear on your news feed. Don't let peer pressure take you away from your goals.

Given the points discussed above, try to become an independent thinker. Don't let the influence of others govern your own actions. Let go of all that and let the contents of this book influence your judgment. It's worked for many others, so why shouldn't it work for you?

Some students react to my advice by saying I want them to turn into workaholic nerds. That's massively far from the truth. I'm encouraging you to be strong minded, not to follow the crowd and make the most of your time – trust me, it will benefit you in the future!

Chapter 10: Step 3 - Motivation...Getting to the table and staying there

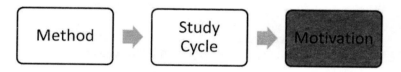

This chapter will show you <u>how</u> to increase your work rate through analysing your day-to-day habits, learning effective motivation techniques and dealing with de-motivating thoughts. After completing this chapter you should be able to fight off procrastination and motivate yourself to study during evenings and weekends.

I am aware there is an array of educational and self-help information on this topic. However, I aim to stay away from the ideas that are useless for students and knuckle down into the methods that work.

What is motivation?

Motivation is a word that is thrown around a lot. I believe motivation to be the inner conscious drive that helps you turn a thought or an idea into action. The opposing force to motivation is procrastination. This is the tendency to 'put off' your actions to a later time.

Boosting Motivation and Destroying Procrastination

Motivation and procrastination should be discussed together because they are like Yin and Yang. When you are highly motivated you tend to procrastinate less and when you are procrastinating a lot then it probably means you are low on motivation. All of us have good days (when motivation is high) and bad days when (procrastination is high). I asked several students to describe their good and bad days to see if there were any common characteristics. A lad called Fawaz gave an answer which pretty much encompassed the responses from everyone else. Here's what he said...

Example of a good study day (Motivation > Procrastination)

"I woke up well rested, feeling quite upbeat and positive. Making a to-do list the night before helped me feel confident about the day ahead. This was because there was some kind of game plan; I felt less uncertain and doubtful. I was still worried about exams but this was keeping me on my toes."

"At school, a guy from the year above told me his success story and it gave me more confidence; if he could do it so could I. This coupled with the positive start made me want to study and I therefore

actively looked for moments during the day where I could get started"

"When it finally came to starting, it wasn't a problem and it didn't take long to get momentum on my side. My mind was firmly focused on what I had to do in the present moment and I wasn't dwelling on the past or worrying about the future. It kind of felt like I was on 'autopilot"

"Naturally I became stuck on some questions and got distracted every so often. However, the desire to complete my goals was strong enough to continuously bring me back to the table"

"This momentum continued when I got home from school and I finished the day strong"

Example of a bad study day (Procrastination > Motivation)

"I had been quite productive over the past few days so woke up feeling good but slightly complacent. Over the course of the day this complacency turned into over confidence and I wasn't really thinking about studying even when the chance presented itself."

"Eventually, when I got home, I decided to sit at my desk and continue from yesterday. I looked through the list of things needed to be done and felt quite overwhelmed. For some reason this got me into a bad mood and therefore, I had trouble concentrating."

"Nevertheless I continued... that's until I got stuck on a practice question. This just added to my frustration. It was a relatively simple question. I lost my confidence and felt insecure about the exam. If I can't do this how am I supposed to do all the other harder questions and pass?"

"The negative thoughts started snow balling. What if I don't get good grades? How embarrassing will it be telling my family and friends if I get poor grades? If I don't pull this off will it ruin everything? I then decided to go and eat some food."

"Two hours had passed and I was still reading over the same page of the text book. After convincing myself that I wasn't in the mood to work, I left to watch TV and didn't return for the rest of the evening."

Good days > bad days = higher grades

What Fawaz described above was his typical 'good day' and 'bad day'. It's important to remember that GCSEs are a marathon not a sprint. Therefore, over 250 or so school days, the people who have more good days and less bad days will probably get better grades – it is simple as that! Before finding out how to boost your good days, I'd like you to follow what Fawaz did; think of any recent good/bad days and make a list of their key characteristics. Fawaz made his own list as shown below:

Characteristics of a Good Day
Positive
Confident – Game plan in place
Feel exam pressure
Heard a success story – it's not impossible
Auto Pilot – Being in the present
Set theme for the day – Set goals early
Un-phased by setback and getting stuck

Characteristics of a Bad Day
Complacent
Over Confident
Overwhelmed – suddenly realising a lot to do.
Frustrated
Insecure - Negative Thoughts
Easily put off by setbacks

Making this list will help you understand your own habits. As you mull over your bad days you will probably realise that they are caused by similar triggers. You may also think of days where you started off well but it all changed when something unexpected happened. When this happens, always try your best to finish the day strong regardless of the setbacks you've experienced during your bad day.

Hopefully now you have an idea of the habits and thoughts which shape how your day goes.

How to have more good study days

In step two of the three step plan we established what the study cycle was and split it into three elements: Intent, Action and Maintenance. Here's a reminder...

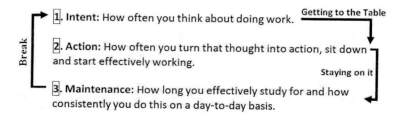

If you're reading this book, then you undoubtedly have plenty of intent and probably think about studying a great deal. After all it's easy to think about what you should be doing. However, acting on your intentions is harder and requires a greater amount of will power and energy. Let me ask you, after you've sat down at your desk and pushed through the first 5-10 minutes, doesn't it feel a lot easier to keep going? The graph below shows how each element of the study cycle require different levels of mental energy.

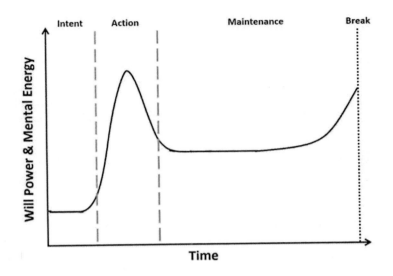

After getting over the first hump, it becomes much easier to concentrate for 15-20 minutes. As you start coming to the end of your attention span, it becomes harder to concentrate and you may need a break. This is how your mind operates during the study cycle and understanding this will help you. Remind yourself of this graph every time you feel like putting off studying. It's only the first 5-10 minutes which are difficult!

Now that you fully understand <u>what</u> the study cycle is, we are ready to learn <u>how</u> we can be effective in executing each of the three elements. The methods described below will help improve your cycle and make it run smoother. Let's start with discussing the most important technique in my opinion – goal setting.

Goal setting (the proper way)

[Target study cycle elements: **1**, **2** and **3**]

Goal setting is a way to define exactly what you want to motivate yourself to do. This is a powerful process for thinking about your ideal future, and for motivating yourself to turn this into reality. I'm going to provide a new perspective on effective goal setting. Let's first get the 4 main rules out of the way...

4 golden rules

Each goal should be...

1. Written down

It's important to note that your mind can easily twist, bend and extend goals as time goes by. Writing something down affirms it and makes it tangible. Therefore, to change that goal would mean physically crossing it out or throwing it in the bin. Not the most comfortable thing to do!

If you wake up to read 'I will get a minimum of six 8s in my GCSEs' every morning, you are more likely to try to feel bad when you sacrifice studying for TV or a night out.

2. Clear

The goal should be so clear that you know immediately whether you have successfully accomplished it. A pass or fail statement such as 'complete 25 practice questions in my maths text book – by 15:00' is much more defined than 'work on maths for rest of the day'. Keep them black and white.

3.   Made with a plan and deadline

"A dream is just a dream. A goal is a dream with a plan and a deadline"
-Anonymous

Having a plan and deadline will provide structure to the goal. It will make it real and prevent you from doubting your ability to achieve goals on time. Remember back to Fawaz's description of his good day? He mentioned that knowing the game plan helped him feel confident and ultimately played a part in having a 'good day'.

4.   Realistic

There is no point setting yourself unrealistic goals because you will constantly under achieve and feel disheartened. The goal should be ambitious but within reach so that you are able to follow it through and gain confidence from completing it.

Try and stick to these rules so you can get the most out of your goals. Now let's talk about setting goals across time frames...

Goal time frames

Goal setting across multiple time frames will help improve all three elements of your Study Cycle...

Time Frame	Time Span	Example
Long	Years	"I will achieve at least seven 8s in my GCSEs by this time next year"
Medium	Weeks/Days	"Complete 1st layer for Biology by two weeks from today"
Short	Hours	"Practice questions 1 to 5 – by 14:00"

113

Long-term goals

These should be set before the start of each academic year and never change. Even now, after university and starting my business, all the long-term goals I've ever made are printed out and still stuck on my wall...

I will achieve 3A's in my A-levels by June 2006 √

I will achieve a first Class Honours in my Degree by June 2009 √

I will be accepted on to an Internship Program at an Investment Bank by June 2009 √

I will write a book to show A-level students how to improve their grades by December 2013 √

I will write a book to show GCSE students how to improve their grades by March 2015 √

I will write a book to show students how to succeed at university by January 2017

Every time a goal was achieved I would draw a large tick on the page. If a goal expired without me achieving it, I either extended it or wrote a new one. I recommend doing the same: write or print your long-term goals out in large, bold font on A4 paper. Then stick them up right in front of your desk.

Finally, give yourself a small print or a disclaimer on those goals to help keep the goal fresh, something like:

I know this goal will try and fade away over time but I must fight to keep it close.

Ace Tips

It is all well and good writing what you want on a piece of paper. However, to really be effective you have to work hard inside your mind. You must really want to do well and achieve the goals you set.

One university student I was mentoring explained, at the start of the academic year, that he wanted to achieve a First Class Honors in his degree. He took my advice and wrote this goal down and pinned it up in his work area. At the end of his academic year and after his last exam I asked him how he got on and he replied "Ye OK...should have passed." This clearly showed that at some point during the year his goal changed from 70% (First Class) to 40% (A Pass). A person who really wanted a First would have been kicking and screaming over the possibility of not achieving what he/she set out to do.

Medium-term goals

Goals across weeks and days will help you piece together the long-term plan. Set the goals to give you some room to manoeuvre in case it takes longer than expected. Once these goals are set you can gauge whether you are working hard enough to complete layers in time for the exam and adjust your time accordingly.

Earlier, Fawaz mentioned that a bad day can be caused by feeling overwhelmed by the amount of work to be done. Having medium-term goals on paper will help attenuate these feelings because it will show a realistic and achievable plan.

As a final note, when setting goals for the day it is best to get your least favourite pieces of work out of the way first when you're fresh and motivation is high. It will help you build momentum and continue on with the rest of the days goals.

For goals in any time frame, sharing them with your parents or friends makes you accountable for getting them done. This is an effective way of motivating yourself to achieve what you set out to do. This uses our inherent nature to compete and feel better than others and can be demonstrated by my treadmill analogy...

Have you ever had a complete stranger jump on a treadmill next to you while in the gym? Did you instinctively feel the need to run faster and longer than them? Studies have shown that most people react in this competitive way. In fact competitiveness is magnified when you go for a run with a friend or someone you know. The same can be applied to academic study. However, as studying is an individual task, you have to create the competition yourself!

This can be done using a weekly e-mail. For example, every Monday you and a friend can send each other's goals for the week ahead and evaluate the week at the end. Even though your mates won't say anything or judge you if you are slacking, a natural competitive tendency will want you to be better than them. The mere thought of someone else knowing your underachievement and even the act of lying about it will be uncomfortable. Furthermore, if you haven't completed any of your goals at the end of the week, you'll feel a bit pants and should hopefully try to push yourself further the next week.

Short-term goals – The goal achieving junky

[Target study cycle elements: **3**]

Here we are going to talk about how to 'stay in the present moment' and focus on the task at hand. The name 'goal achieving junky', as strange it may sound, is exactly the type of idea I want to promote to you. I want you to open your mind to becoming a short-term results driven addict. Someone who not only makes goals and pushes to achieve them, but also craves the feeling of achieving them again and again.

This isn't really a technique of any sort but more just a change in attitude or habit. Start scribbling down or typing out goals regularly. These can be on paper, post it notes or on your phone.

During our research we found that many successful students wrote multiple reminders of their short and long-term goals all over the place, from their bedroom to their bathroom! It also helps to physically tick or cross them off when they are complete.

This works because you associate 'good behaviour' with a positive result. Just like how you give a dog a treat if he sits when you ask him to! Working hard would be equivalent to 'good behaviour' and hitting the target/crossing it off the page would be the positive stimulus. This will help you achieve three things:

1. Help you work effectively for longer
2. Encourage you to drive for results and finish tasks through rather than leaving them unfinished
3. Provide continuous results that you will feel good about, and therefore help keep your mind fully focused on the task at hand

Remember you have to approach studying like how an athlete would with his physical training or how an Olympian would push themselves by thinking one more rep or one more lap, you have to think one more page or one more goal.

Self bribery

[Target study cycle elements: **2** and **3**]

Sounds a bit childish right? But bribing yourself is a useful way of providing that extra little bit of motivation to hit your short time-frame targets. This will help you become a more results driven person who looks forward to finishing tasks thoroughly and detests leaving things half way. Bribes and treats can also be incorporated into the goals you set at the start of the day. For example:

Last 10 pages of Macbeth = 15 min break and sandwich snack
First 20 questions of algebra = 30 min – Game of Thrones

Make sure the treats you choose don't let you get carried away and cause you to waste more time than you accounted for. When you are taking a break it is much easier to say 10 more minutes of TV then it is to say 10 more minutes of biology.

Below are 5 of the best & worst things that you can do during your break. You'll see that even though the 'worst' may seem more fun, they will deter you from getting back to revision. You need to give yourself treats according to the time of day and how much work you've done

5 best:
1. Short burst of intensive exercise - 10 min sit ups
2. Short walk or fresh air
3. Small snack
4. Shower
5. Short TV programme

5 worst:
1. Heavy meal
2. Starting a movie
3. Shopping

4. YouTube

5. PS3, Xbox or other games console

High impact – high reward

[Target study cycle elements: **1** and **2**]

Have you ever experienced a period of time where you just couldn't build any momentum? Every time you attempted to work, it all goes square and nothing gets done? Me too.

The damage comes when the 'slow patch' continues and then becomes the norm or a habit. Therefore, it's important to be aware of when it happens and to take action. Taking action can sometimes be hard, but, with three simple steps, you should be able to get over the hill.

> Step one: Recognise whether something is a one off or if it is turning into a spiralling habit.

> Step two: Have the discipline to make a personal change to break that habit. The longer you leave it running the harder it will be to break.

> Step three: Take action by doing something out of your comfort zone, i.e. something you would not normally do.

I remember after successfully completing my mid-year exams I decided to take a break for 2 weeks. Following a few nights out, I attempted to build momentum and get back into the routine. I was too complacent and it just wasn't happening. This continued for another 2 weeks until a friend helped me realise that continuing in this way will undo all my hard work in the first term. I'm glad I took the break because I deserved and needed it, but I had to find a way to get back into routine...

As an arguable 'punishment' for myself I took my books, told my girlfriend to leave me alone for a couple of days, got my mum to take my phone, drop me to my grandma's house and just leave me there for a few days. Looking back makes me both cringe and chuckle. My grandma was a very spiritual lady who meditated for hours on end. I hoped that by staying there, I could soak up some of that spirituality and it would somehow help me break out of my cycle. Ridiculous – I know! It felt like I was going on my very own revision spiritual retreat and guess what? It worked! While I didn't turn into a meditating teenager, over those few days I worked efficiently, hit all my goals and got right back on track.

Back then I was kind of spooked and thought perhaps the spirituality actually helped me change course. In hindsight, it was the random shift in environment, boredom (no TV) and early starts because my grandma kept waking me up with all her bell ringing and chanting. Regardless, the whole experience knocked some sense into me and got me right back on course.

Motivational springboard

[Target study cycle elements: **1 and 3**]

Have you ever been really motivated by an inspiring person before? I'm sure you have. Their ideas, opinions, charisma and inspirational language can provide a real motivation boost especially if you're having a 'bad day'. It's unfortunate we can't experience that 'umph!' all the time because we naturally have low periods every now and again. Well you can't read a motivational piece of text every time you feel less motivated right? Well, why not!? There are hundreds of books, websites, YouTube videos, Facebook pages, celebrity biographies etc which you can use to give a quick boost when feeling de-motivated. Use these as a spring board to get yourself out of a period of low motivation. However beware, don't use this as an excuse to procrastinate!

David Attenborough is in my head

[Target study cycle elements: **3**]

This is a weird albeit effective technique for when you are close to hitting your target but running low on concentration. To grab those last few minutes of your attention span, use your mind to narrate the information in your text book using someone else's voice. This could be anyone's voice but personally I like using David Attenborough! I find his voice quite distinctive and it makes me want to listen to what he's saying. Have a go – no harm in trying!

Ejection seat (coming close to something then bailing at the last moment)

[Target study cycle elements: **2**]

This little trick can help you avoid procrastination. It should be used when you know you need to start working and there is something you are really tempted to do such as watch TV, read a magazine, or play a video game. Bring yourself really close to doing it then bail at the last minute – like how a fighter pilot ejects before crashing. The more emphatically you do this the better! For example, if you want to watch TV, then go towards the remote, pick it up, point it at the TV but then suddenly and emphatically chuck on to the sofa. Then turn around immediately and go to your desk! This might be hard or seem a bit weird, but try it, it works!

Summary so far...

The methods described so far in step 3 were those I've used personally. I understand that some of them sound strange. In fact, when I started mentally narrating my Chemistry textbook in David Attenborough's voice, I thought I was going a bit loony. However, being a little crazy can be helpful and sometimes necessary! We need to do whatever it takes to make the arduous task of studying more interesting.

Dealing with the devil on your shoulder

No matter how positive you try to be, we're only human so negative thoughts can and will enter your mind. It's normal to have the devil on your shoulder making you worry and the angel reassuring you that things will be ok. However, what if the devils badgering just becomes too much for you? What if his voice overpowers the angels? This can sometimes result in a negative de-motivating spiral that can hold you back from achieving your goals.

De-motivating thoughts

Our minds are complex things that scientists still know very little about. All we know is that our actions are influenced by our thoughts and emotions. Controlling our emotions to benefit us is a skill that some do better than others. However, through understanding and practice, you can bring order to the chaos.

Earlier we saw how, after falling into a bad mood and experiencing a setback, Fawaz spiralled from being confident to insecure. He stopped thinking about the present moment and started worrying about the future. Eventually this made him unproductive, feel too overwhelmed and he gave up. We can never completely avoid bad days like this but we can limit them simply by monitoring and understanding our de-motivating thoughts. The key is to remember that these thoughts are emotional and are caused by irrationality.

In my research three core psychological issues with revision continuously pop up: lack of self-belief, fear of failure and inability to see immediate results. In this section I will outline the best solutions to tackle them.

Lack of self-belief –"I'm not good enough to…"

You hear parents and coaches tell their kids in Hollywood sports movies all the time 'Believe in yourself son'. What does this mean? Let's break it down.

Self-belief is the trust in your ability to accomplish what you set out to do. Without it, achieving your goals becomes impossible because you'll believe they are unattainable regardless of what you do or how hard you work.

Why do people have low self-belief?

The most common examples of why people have low self-belief are intelligence, quality of school, past results, low attention span and difficulty with self-motivation. You may have a smarter older brother/sister/cousin who makes you feel stupid. You may constantly be compared to family members or friends. These are misconceptions and have to be proactively addressed to accomplish your goal.

Drilling even deeper, everyone is insecure on some level because our minds are wired in that way. A little insecurity can keep you on your toes but, a lot of it can hold you back from achieving what you want.

I know this because I hit the lowest low after seeing my AS results. On the surface, I blamed everything. For example I blamed my teachers. However, deep down, I blamed my own attributes. I was convinced that my poor grades were mostly down to the low intelligence that I inherited from my parents. As I mentioned earlier, I even suggested that I had some sort of attention-deficit disorder. Eventually, I realised how irrational these thoughts were, but it wasn't enough to keep them at bay.

There were moments where I believed in my ability, but these were followed by long periods where I would think 'Who am I kidding? What are the chances of actually pulling this off?' This was evidence that I didn't truly believe I could get the grades I wanted. If I stood any chance of turning this situation around, I had to come up with some solution.

Solution:

Firstly, keep an open mind when it comes to your own ability; just remember many others have experienced the same lack of self-belief. On their own, they came to realise how irrational it was and still succeeded.

Secondly, if you have hit rock bottom then I want you to embrace that and let yourself be bitter about being there. Feel 'comfortably pissed off' by the situation and understand that from this point onwards you have absolutely nothing to lose. Snarl at your grades and have the audacity to challenge yourself to achieve. Say to yourself, I want a full set of 8s through whatever means necessary. Dismiss any thought of damage control suggesting you should try and salvage some 5's and 4's. Why aim for mediocre when you can be the best? Affirm the following:

'Life is too short to just sit and accept my short comings. I'm going to attempt the so called 'impossible'. I'm going to throw everything I have at these exams. If I don't get what I want, only then will I accept that I am not cut out for this. These commitments I'm making will try to fade over time but I must fight to keep them close'

The affirmation above was one I constantly said out loud to myself. It enabled me to experience that quite sudden paradigm shift where I turned into a highly effective person. Execute the suggestions in this book, and you can do the same!

Fear – 'What if...'

The emotion of fear exists to help us steer clear of unfavourable experiences. Our minds constantly run through different scenarios that we are fearful of, which is why we constantly ask ourselves 'What if...'

When you're afraid, even if you've decided to take on a challenge, a part of you is determined to avoid going forward. This slows you down and makes you careful, which is useful. However, sometimes your fears are based on your imagination rather than an accurate assessment of the risks in your reality.

Even if you have a strong desire to move forward, the 'safety' emotion of fear will kick in and prevent you from working at your best.

For students we found the most common fear was:

How would my
parents react?

What if I don't
get into college?

What if I can't
get into
university?

What if I fail?

What if I have to
redo the year?

What if I ruin
my future?

Such fears will keep you on your toes and help improve all three elements of your study cycle.

The destructive fear factor

In many cases, fear can be such a strong emotion that it becomes demoralising. This is especially true if you've tasted failure before and are worried that it may happen again. If untreated this can manifest into a destructive emotion and de-motivate you because it's such a bitter pill to swallow if you don't succeed. In our research, 76% of students mentioned that a fear of failure hindered their performance instead of helping.

Solution:

Ideally, every time we have an aggressive fear, we should follow the flow chart below...

Fear Flow Chart

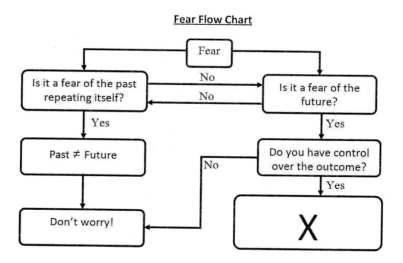

Obviously, this is easier said than done!

If you're wondering if that 'X' in the flow chart is an error, it isn't! It's just to represent the only <u>variable</u> in the flow chart. Before talking about variable 'X' let's talk about the two things we can't change i.e. the constants...

1. Fearing the past will repeat itself - There is no such thing as a run of bad luck. People believe in nonsense like this because the human brain creates patterns out of random events, discards contradicting evidence and remembers the events that fit the pattern. Unfortunately for most of us, the hurt of losing is more memorable than the euphoria of winning. You have to flip this on its head. Try adopting a short-term memory when it comes to bad experiences from the past and a long-term memory for your successes.

2. Worrying or being scared of a future scenario that you cannot control is a waste of time. This is because there is no way to predict the future. Understand that the way it plays out in your mind is only imagination and is far from reality. Keep reminding yourself of this fact.

You have all the tools, so let's talk about variable 'X'...

If you have debilitating fears of certain scenarios or outcomes occurring in the future, that you can control, (like your GCSE results) then there are steps you can take to help. Firstly, the best way is to have an effective plan in place that you believe in. If you understand and execute the methods discussed in this book, particularly within the '3 steps', you will begin to see your fears fade. The methods in 'Step 1' will help you absorb information more effectively. Noticing your work ethic improve will naturally shift your sight from fear of failure to euphoria of success. This is exactly what I experienced.

Early on in school, I was constantly in fear. What if I don't finish my revision on time? What if I run out of time in the exam? What if I go in and I forget everything?

When I got my act together, these fears were still lingering around but it was easy to push them aside. This was because I believed my plan would work and, while executing it, I could see evidence it was working. When it finally came to exams, I remember thinking that I'd given myself the best possible chance to succeed and there wasn't much more I could do. After this point I entered the exam hall confident and, most importantly, fearless.

Remind yourself that there have been many others in your position, who have felt the same demoralising fear and conquered it to significantly improve their grades.

As a final note, by succumbing to our fears, we end up cordoning off large areas of our own ability. Life is inescapably risky and painful, not to mention 100% fatal. So don't feel you can dodge a bit of pain by backing down from something a bit scary. Face your fears and go for it!

Inability to see immediate results

Most things worth achieving usually take a lot of time and effort. GCSEs are no different. For both years there are approximately 9 months from the point you receive your syllabus to the point of your exams. Each time I started a school year, I vividly remember feeling like exams were still so far away. I didn't really address the possibility that I'd leave it too late and was coasting through the year thinking everything will kind of sort itself out. I'd say to myself 'I'll start working hard soon'. Of course soon came too late and there wasn't enough time to do a good amount of layers.

Once I remember attempting to sit at the table to revise for a physics module. The script and conversation in my head went more or less like this:

"oh look its 7:30pm maybe I should go over some physics"

I sit down at the table, stare at my text book and 5 minutes later...

"This is pretty hard, maybe I'll watch TV for a bit – there are still a few weeks left so what is half an hour going to change anyway? I'll concentrate after"

I go watch TV and half an hour turns into an hour, an hour turns into 2 hours and low and behold I never return till the next evening when the same thing happens again.

The complacency of knowing there was ample time before an exam prevented me from actually getting started. At the time I thought half an hour here or there would contribute very little to achieving my final grade. This was probably true <u>if it was just a one off</u>. However, because I let myself get away with it so many times, it became a bad habit. Now the problem was that lots of time was lost and this cycle could have been corrected by a proactive approach to the issue.

Solution:

It dawned on me then that being an effective person is all about how you condition yourself. It's about proactively producing that deadline pressure on your own, not reacting late to external forces. It's important to understand that you need to make a sacrifice now for what you want eventually.

The most fundamental way of making this happen is by setting your own deadlines in advance of those that are given to you. After making my proactive plan, I finished the first layer for some of my exams before my teachers got round to teaching them. In fact I used the classroom lessons as a second layer and not so surprisingly, these were the modules I hit the highest grades in. In addition to setting your own deadlines, if you find yourself constantly justifying your procrastination by the amount of time there is, then it is important to focus on the process rather than the result. This can be explained by the wall analogy:

"You don't set out to build a wall. You don't say 'I'm going to build the biggest, baddest, greatest wall that's ever been built.' You don't start there. You say, 'I'm going to lay this brick as perfectly as a brick can be laid. You do that every single day. And soon you have a wall."
-- Will Smith

The individual who stays at the table, absorbs the most information and does the most layers will get the better grade. Just how a footy team that wins the most and loses the least number of matches wins the league. Each day should be seen as an important match. You will have some missed matches, with surprise defeats and some draws but, overall if you keep winning the result will present itself at the end. From this point onwards, think of yourself as an academic athlete rather than a student.

When it comes to forgetting the result and concentrating on the process there is no better advice than to be a short-term goal setting junky. Keep jotting down goals and deadlines. This way you can create your own little victories every day and become immersed in the process.

Onwards and upwards...

Chapter 11: What A-Levels shall I pick?

In year 11, you will have to pick your BTEC or A-level subjects and start applying to colleges and 6thforms. There will be a lot of advice thrown at you from all over the place. Many will say *"Make sure you choose subjects that you are interested in!"* Yes, your interest in the subject does matter, but there are a few more questions you need to ask yourself before submitting your final selection...

Already know what you want to do after university?

If you have a clear passion for a subject and know what you want to pursue for a career, first find out what degree you will need to apply for at university. Then browse through the prospectuses of the universities offering the course you want and check what A-levels they require. Usually it's quite obvious and universities ask for 1 or 2 specific A-level subjects. For example, Medicine and dentistry usually require Biology and/or Chemistry A-levels.

If you don't have a clue what you want to do with your life yet, then <u>it's best to pick subjects which you enjoy and are likely to succeed in.</u>

Are you a 'Mathsy', 'Wordy', 'Arty' or 'Languagey' person?

Mathsy (or Sciencey)...

...people are better at problem solving and using numbers in comparison to analysing texts and writing essays. A mathsy person usually performs better at fact recall and method and understanding subjects like Maths or the sciences.

If you're a total mathsy person and tend to struggle with written prose essays, then I recommend sticking to subjects that require non-essay short answers in exams. These include subjects like Mathematics, Further Mathematics, Physics, Biology, Chemistry, Geography and ICT.

Occasionally, you may find that 2 or more of these subjects contain topics which overlap. Physics and Maths are a typical example. This makes it easier when it comes to revision and gives you a better chance of achieving good grades in both subjects.

Wordy...

...students tend to enjoy reading in their own time and have a bias towards English type subjects. If you think you are wordy then ask yourself: am I good at analysing texts, forming opinions and reading between the lines? Am I good at translating these opinions into free flowing written English?

If the answer's yes, then you have a lot of options. The most obvious being English which is the most popular A-level qualification in the UK. Subjects like Law, Psychology, Politics and Sociology also contain a fair deal of essay writing. If you truly are a 'wordy' then it's good to have a bias for these subjects when selecting your A-levels as taking too many 'Mathsy' subjects may become cumbersome...

vic @vic_vic_marie Mar 23
I kind of wish I'd picked more **essay based subjects** instead of mostly exam **based** ones

shan @_ShannonWood May 7
Essay based subjects like English, history and sociology are no problem for me but math and science is like a different language

If the answer's a maybe or no, then think carefully before choosing a subject which requires a lot of essay writing. Every year, I receive messages and see tweets like these...

lauraa @Lauraaa_Martinn Mar 24
Don't take four **essay based subjects** if you can't write essays lol

ily zayn @_heyitsphoebe Mar 24
why did i choose three **subjects** where the exams are all **based** on **essay based** questions WHY

Soph @Sophie_Loaderr Mar 15
Thing is it's only after taking all essay based subjects have I realised I can't actually write essays well at all

george @___georgebirch Jun 3
I'm taking four **essay based subjects** next year and I'm the world's slowest writer oops

Many of these students had genuine interests in subjects like History and Law. They were able to memorise the facts and form opinions on the subjects too. However, they struggled to structure their opinions and facts properly, and get it down on paper fast enough. I had the same issue too and finishing on time was always difficult because my writing was so stop and start. It's hard enough recalling the facts sometimes, let alone thinking about structure, spelling, grammar and vocabulary.

Also, is your hand writing any good? Improving your handwriting will be difficult at this age so if your writing is illegible then you're already on the back foot. You may need to write very quickly in written prose exams so this can become a problem if the quality of your handwriting becomes worse the faster you write.

Arty...

...people have a knack for sketching, painting and graphics. Do you find yourself casually doodling on pieces of paper and then receiving loads of compliments for it? Did you do Art for GCSE and receive good marks for your work? If yes, then it may not be a bad move, particularly if you're someone who freezes up in exams.

Languagey...

Taking a foreign language at A-level, can reap huge rewards in the future but only if you carry it through to university. It opens up your options because many universities combine top degrees with languages. For example, you can study law with French or economics with German. You can even opt to do a year abroad which will just be awesome and improve your language skills further.

Sticking to a language right through university will pay off when you start applying for jobs. When I was applying for graduate positions at investment banks, many of the best high paying jobs either required or preferred a second language. Many of my university friends who were fluent or studied a language, received job offers a lot more easily.

Remember, only pick a language if you know for sure that you have an aptitude for it and want to follow through with it to university. If you're not, in my opinion you're better off picking a fact recall subject which is easier to achieve a top grade in.

No preference...

If you are indifferent to any subject or are good at 2 or more areas then keep a bias towards subjects with short answer questions (Maths and sciences). Contrary to wordy essay long answer type subjects, these exams have clearly defined mark schemes. This means the opinion of the examiner marking your paper is irrelevant and they can only mark you based on what the mark scheme says.

What exam boards do your prospective colleges and 6th forms use for the subjects you are interested in?

Once you have shortlisted the subjects you like, contact each college or 6th form you are applying to and find out what exam boards they use for the specific subjects that you are interested in. Either by asking the colleges or checking the exam board websites, find out the following:

1. Have the specifications stayed the same for that subject for several years?
2. Is there an up to date textbook available for that subject which will still be relevant when you start the subjects?
3. If the syllabus is changing will a new up to date textbook be issued for the new syllabus?

From the 'Verify your textbook' section in chapter 8b, it's clear to see how much of a difference an up-to-date textbook makes to your chances of achieving top grades. Having a verified textbook will mean you don't need to piece together learning material or even worry about taking notes in class. It will make your life easier over the next 2 years.

You also want a specification that hasn't changed in a long time because the exams become more predictable.

Chapter 12: Don't forget to be a kid!

This is the last chapter and therefore my last chance to pass on some useful advice to you! Over the past few chapters, we have attacked GCSEs and exams from every angle. It's clear that studying and the road to achieving good grades can be quite solitary. A lot of time will be spent in your house on your own looking over your books. This cycle of solitary studying can be quite damaging for some, particularly those who prefer keeping to themselves. This is why it's so important to get out of the house every so often to engage in activities which are not so solitary. Everyone may go on at you about achieving good grades but having a social life is just as important. Don't forget to be a kid!

Spending time with friends is a great way to put all the serious stuff aside for a moment and just enjoy being responsibility free. The stories you make with your friends will be told again and again. In fact, I still tell others about how my friends and I removed all the furniture from another mate's living room and rearranged it in his back garden. Having laughs like this keeps you sane, but it's also important to participate in extracurricular social activities. Doing so will develop your **social confidence.**

What is social confidence? Jennifer Lawrence, Will Smith, Jeremy Clarkson, Barack Obama. These are all individuals with excellent social confidence. They are full of energy, stories and have mastered the art of conversation. 'Well obviously because they are celebrities' you might say. Were they born celebrities? No, they developed their social skills by continuously stepping out of their comfort zones and putting themselves under pressure. You should do this too! Here's how...

Building social confidence

Firstly, speak to as many different types of people from all walks of life. Have conversations with individuals a few years older to get an idea of what you'll be thinking about later down the line. Mentor those a few years younger to learn how far you've come. The world is now very international so speak to people from different countries to understand other cultures.

Secondly, continuously step outside your comfort zone. This can be done through extra-curricular activities like playing music or competitive sport. I'm not talking about playing guitar in your room or a kick about at lunch time. I'm taking about performing in front of people or playing in a competitive league. Doing so will also help you perform under pressure and build your character.

Thirdly, put yourself out there and do something different. Start a YouTube channel or a blog. Start a business or social enterprise. Do some travelling, volunteer or charity work. Fitting in these activities alongside the layered learning time table can be difficult. However with efficient learning techniques and good time management, anything's possible.

Best of luck with all your future endeavours!

Appendix 1: Table comparing traditional note taking to the scribble technique.

For arguments sake let's say you have 3 weeks total to learn for a specific exam. The percentages below were calculated through our own research and may not apply to everyone.

		Traditional Note Taking	Scribble Technique
Week 1 - Rep 1	Time	This first repetition will take relatively long because notes have to be both neatly written and accurate. Also, as the material will be new and un-familiar. Rate of learning = 12 sides an hour.	Similar to traditional note taking, fresh and unfamiliar material will impact the time required to complete this repetition. However, reading, closing the book and scribbling will be quite a fast process. Rate of learning = 10 sides an hour.
	Retention	I have now made notes equating to approx. 70% of the total information in the text book. Of this let's say I can retain 30% of my notes so the net retention of the textbook is 21% (30% of 70%). This declines quite rapidly over time.	I've studied in detail through 100% of the total information in the text book. Of this I can retain 40% and the net retention is 40%. This declines relatively slowly over time.
Week 2 -Rep2	Time	Naturally, the 2nd rep is faster because the information is familiar and I'm focusing more on learning than writing neatly. Rate of learning = 15 sides an hour.	Even though a lot of information was covered on the first rep, each page I turn to is familiar. Therefore this rep is much faster. Rate of learning = 15 sides an hour.
	Retention	I'm retaining a lot more. My notes cover 70% of the text book and I am retaining 60% of my notes. Net retention = 42%.	The 2nd layer of information means I'm retaining 20% more information. This means I'm retaining 60% of the text book. Net retention = 60%.

| Week 3 - Rep 3 | Time | Now I'm just reading over my notes and highlighting/re-writing bits I keep forgetting. Learning rate = 20 sides an hour. | This 3rd rep is much faster. All I'm doing is skimming over the pages and only covering/scribbling parts that are not familiar. Learning rate = 20 sides an hour |
| | Retention | Covering the material a 3rd time means I now retain 80% of my notes from 70% of the syllabus. Net retention = 56%. | A 3rd layer has boosted my retention up another 10% and I can pretty much remember 70% of the text book. This doesn't mean I can re-write it word for word but most exam questions I could quite easily remember enough points to get full marks. Net retention = 70%. |

Other titles available

Available amazon.co.uk